Using a Map and Compass

DON GEARY

STACKPOLE
BOOKS

Published by
STACKPOLE BOOKS
5067 Ritter Road
Mechanicsburg, PA 17055

Printed in the United States of America

10 9 8 7 6 5 4 3 2 1

First edition

Cover design by Caroline Miller

Library of Congress Cataloging–in–Publication Data

Geary, Don.
    Using a map and compass / Don Geary. — 1st ed.
      p.cm.
    ISBN0–8117–2591–X (pbk. : alk. paper)
    1. Orienteering—United States. I. Title.
    GV200.4.G43 1995
    796.5'1—dc20   95–3069
                                       CIP

• CONTENTS •

• ACKNOWLEDGMENTS •

I would like to thank Byron Williams for doing a number of the illustrations in this book. I would also like to thank Hal Heron, President of the Brunton Compass Company and the folks at Cabela's, Pur (water filters), MPI, and Magellan.

• INTRODUCTION •

Every year, especially during the warmer months, hundreds of thousands of people take to the hills in pursuit of outdoor recreation. The statistics from outdoor equipment manufacturers are mind-boggling. For example, in 1991 American anglers spent more than $15 million on fishing lures alone, a mere trifle in light of the cost of backpacks, sleeping bags, tents, firearms, and even gasoline used in the quest of the great outdoors.

Many of these people are looking for that hard-to-define place called *wilderness*. Unfortunately, most of them never find truly wild places. Nine out of ten hikers and other wilderness travelers stay on the marked trail systems that cover less than 1 percent of all wilderness areas in the continental United States, and more and more hikers, fishermen, hunters, and mountain bikers take to the trails every season. More people presently use the Lake Placid-Northville Trail (in New York's Adirondack Mountains) during the winter months than did during the entire year just twenty years ago. Sad to say, the wild places themselves are shrinking with every passing year, even in the Rocky Mountain states.

The wilderness is still there, however. Most outdoorsmen just don't know where to look for it. If you have ever listened to a pretrip conversation, it probably went something like this: "Some friends and I are going up to the mountains for a few days of fishing. We're just going to take the freeway to exit 323 and follow the signs to the lake, park the car, and head out. There are plenty of lakes up that way, and we just plan to wander and fish a bunch of them. We have a Forest Service map of the general area, and that's good enough for us." This is a common attitude of today's wilderness travelers. Check out later how the fellows made out. Ask them how their trip went.

You're very likely to get a response like this: "What a trip! It took us an extra six hours to get there because we got lost on those dirt Forest Service roads, and by that time it was too late to get very far in before we had to set up camp. We figured we could make it to a nice lake before setting up camp, but even though we walked longer than we should have, we didn't make it to any lake on the first night. We thought we'd fill our canteens at the trailhead, but someone had backed a horsetrailer over the only spigot, so there was no water, and only one guy had filled his canteen at home.

"Second day we tried to find Big Piney Pond, the one with the monster trout in it. It was supposed to be due north of the trailhead about four miles. I swear we walked about ten hours trying to find that damned pond. We did find a pond that day, but by the time we did, everyone was so tired from breaking trail through the forest that no one even tried fishing. We also discovered that Tom had lost his sleeping pad. It must have pulled off his pack somewhere in the brush.

"The third day we fished the heck out of this pond, but we didn't have any luck. That afternoon we discovered the reason. The pond is on a packhorse trail, just a few hours' ride from the trailhead, and it's where pack trains often spend their first night. Those guys riding horses all day aren't too tired to fish, so the lake gets a lot of fishing pressure. As it turned out, the name of the lake was Pack Horse Pond and not Big Piney.

"A group on horseback came by in the afternoon, and I asked one of the cowboys if he knew where Big Piney Pond was. He showed me on his topo that we were about a mile and a half from it. I checked it out and the bearing was about ninety degrees due east of our position.

"The next day we found the pond, and we all did well in the trout department. Only problem was that the following day was our last day and we had to head back. I sure wish we could have stayed there longer, but it took us more time than we figured to get there. Better luck next time, I guess."

That, I believe, is a fair description of far too many wilderness trips. It took longer than necessary to get to the wilderness in the first place, which ate up valuable time. Poor planning resulted in starting off the hike late and spending the first night with very little water. (If everyone had filled up at home or at least at some point along the way, there would have been plenty of water for the first day.) And most important, the original objective was not reached until the fourth day. Thus poor fishing resulted from poor planning.

The best way to avoid a trip that doesn't live up to your expectations is to learn as much about an area as you possibly can before strapping on your pack. The best source of this type of information is a topographical map of the area. Plan your route, not with an ironclad itinerary, but at least with your basic trip goals in mind.

When you finally get to the edge of the wilderness, use the tools of navigation—a topographical map and a compass—to help you find your way. There really is no such thing as a natural sense of direction; when people are left to wander, they go in circles rather than stay on a straight course.

There are hundreds of lakes and valleys that are visited only by big-game animals, birds, and other woodland creatures—secret and special places that have not suffered from the touch of modern man. These places still exist mainly because no trails lead to them and most people don't spend the time to seek them. All you really need to find these places for yourself are a topographical map and a compass, plus good judgment—for which there is no substitute—and a little determination. It is my hope that this book will help you learn the necessary navigational skills so that you can find a wilderness of your own. I also sincerely hope that when you do find areas that can rightly be considered wilderness, you will walk lightly and leave nothing in passing but the rustling of the leaves.

• ONE •

The Compass

A compass is the basic tool of navigation, and you need to learn to use it before you can expect to travel with any kind of confidence. A compass is not a toy, but a reasonably precise instrument that is invaluable for navigating over land, on the water, or in the air. Learning to use one will enable you not only to navigate, but also to reach predetermined objectives with the confidence that is the true mark of an experienced outdoorsman.

Mastering the compass is not difficult if you understand the basic fundamentals. To begin with, magnetism is the force that makes a compass work. The earth's surface is covered by an invisible magnetic field, which affects, and is affected by, all other magnetic materials on, above, and below it. Picture the earth's axis as a very long bar magnet with north and south poles. All magnetic objects on the earth, if allowed to swing freely, will align themselves with this north-south line. A compass needle will align itself along this line no matter where in the world it is placed.

Early exploration of the globe was accelerated by the discovery of lodestone, a stone with natural magnetic properties.

A compass is a basic navigational tool for wilderness travelers.

(Below) A magnetized needle, pushed through a piece of cork and floated in a bowl of water, will align itself along a north-south axis. This is the underlying principle of the magnetic compass.

Before this discovery, navigators found their way by observing the sun, moon, and stars. The age of exploration really began when the properties of lodestone were put to use. It was discovered, for example, that if a piece of lodestone was suspended so that it could swing freely, it would align itself along a north-south axis. It was later discovered that these same magnetic properties could be transferred to a piece of iron (steel had not yet been invented) simply by rubbing the metal with a piece of lodestone.

The discovery of the properties of lodestone probably occurred in ancient China about the first century B.C. A pivot compass was in use in the West around A.D. 1300, a few years after the return of Marco Polo. One hundred years later a compass was standard equipment on ships voyaging to the New World and exploring the globe.

The modern compass is more refined and easier to use, but the basic principles are exactly the same. The compass has a magnetized needle or card that is allowed to swing freely on

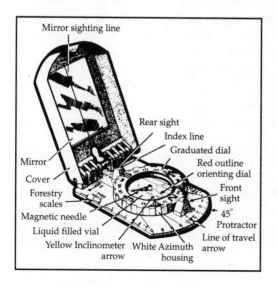

Exploded view of a compass.

some type of pivot. A compass card shows, at the very least, the four compass points of north, south, east, and west. Such things as a damping feature, luminous dial, sights, and a magnetic declination adjusting mechanism may be added for various purposes.

HOW A COMPASS WORKS

A compass needle points to magnetic north, and once north has been established, the direction or bearing to anything in the world can be described by a degree reading. Magnetic north is designated as 0 degrees or 360 degrees. The other cardinal points marked on the compass dial, or rose, are separated by 90 degrees. East is 90 degrees, south is 180 degrees, and west is 270 degrees. Other compass points also have name designations depending on their direction. Northwest, for example, is about 315 degrees and located midway between north and west. North-Northwest is closer to north than west and about 340 degrees. West-Northwest, on the other hand, is closer to west than north and falls at roughly 290 degrees. Other compass points are described in a similar manner—Southwest, for example, is located midway between south and west and is roughly 225 degrees.

The dial on any good compass will be marked in degrees, usually indicated by short lines, called *tick marks*, every 2, 5, or 10 degrees. A compass without degree readings, or only showing the cardinal compass points, is really useless for navigating.

The degree reading or bearing for an objective changes with the point of view. For example, the corner of a house might have a value of 200 degrees when viewed from the center of a room but a different value when viewed from another room or a point outside the house. Readings of specific objects will change whenever the location of the compass has changed.

When using a topographical map and compass, you need to make some adjustments, because all compasses point to magnetic north but all topo maps are oriented to geographical north. The difference between these two points (about 1,300 miles!) is called magnetic declination. Chapter 3 covers magnetic declination in detail.

Almost any metal object can affect how your compass operates. A belt buckle, handgun, sheath knife or pocketknife, rifle, camera, and binoculars are probably the most common offenders. Natural and unavoidable influences include iron deposits in the earth, lightning storms, high-voltage power

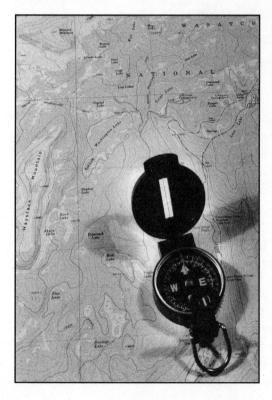

You must adjust for magnetic declination when using a compass and topographical map.

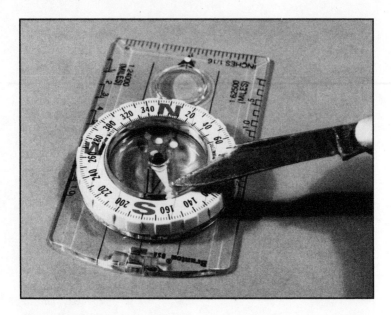

Common metal objects can affect your compass and give you false readings.

lines, and periods of high static electricity in the atmosphere. Even a lit flashlight bulb is a powerful electromagnet that may influence a compass needle or dial. Keep this in mind when traveling in the dark with the aid of a compass and flashlight.

Check for compass interference regularly by watching the action of the compass needle. If your compass needle swings erratically it is being influenced by something other than magnetic north. Even if the compass is equipped with a dampening mechanism or fluid, the action of the needle should not be abrupt. It should swing left and right a few moments before coming to rest.

Probably the best way to determine if your compass is being influenced by other forces is to set it down on a log, the ground, or a rock. It is important that the compass lie flat and that there are no deposits in the area, in a rock for example. (A metal deposit will cause a compass needle to stop abruptly.) Now back a few steps away from the compass and let the needle come to a rest. After a minute or so, slowly move back to the compass, at the same time watching the action of the compass needle. If the needle moves as you approach, something on your person is causing the compass needle to deviate. Remove any metal, such as a metal belt buckle or pocketknife, and try this test again. The things that can affect a compass needle are surprising; even the metal in a ballpoint pen can cause some needle deviation.

CHOOSING A COMPASS

There are four basic types of compasses in use today by outdoor travelers: floating dial, fixed dial, cruiser, and orienteering. All of them indicate direction, but their special features are designed for specific uses. Before buying a compass,

Floating dial compass.

examine your needs and choose the kind that will do the best job for you.

Floating Dial Compasses

Any compass that has a joined compass card and needle that work as a single unit is a floating dial compass. Floating dial compasses include automobile, aircraft, and boat compasses, as well as military surplus and lensatic compasses.

On a ship, the floating dial compass is set in the center of the cockpit or wheelhouse so that the line on the compass housing runs in the same direction as the keel of the ship. This line, called the *lubber line*, indicates the direction of travel, as if the ship were an arrow. The compass dial or card is allowed to swing freely, and the direction of travel is read off the card where the lubber line points.

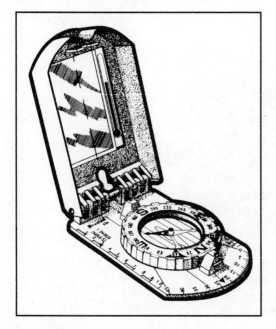

Lensatic compass.

On a lensatic compass, the principle is the same except that a sight is commonly used to pick up an object in the distance. A wire is set into the compass cover, and a V sight is on the other side of the compass housing. An object is sighted in the distance, and the degree reading is noted through a lens below the V sight.

A lensatic compass is not the easiest or quickest to use, because you must hold the compass so that you can see both your objective and the degree reading. This necessitates holding the compass close to your eye, and it leaves a lot of room for error. For this reason, a lensatic compass may not be your best choice for wilderness travel.

Fixed Dial Compasses

Fixed dial compasses are the ones most commonly carried

Fixed dial compass.

and used by outdoorsmen. They are a poor choice, however, because they are not as accurate or easy to operate as other types of compasses. The popularity of the fixed dial compass undoubtedly lies in its low price. Many outdoorsmen reason that they should carry a compass but do not see why they should pay very much money for one.

A fixed dial compass resembles a pocketwatch with a pop-up cover. Inside are a needle and compass card. Few show more than the major compass points, and even fewer are damped to slow needle travel. There is rarely any sighting device or direction-of-travel arrow, so they are suitable only for showing general direction. Fixed dial compasses are one step above a magnetized needle stuck in a cork and floated in a bowl of water. Their operation is very slow and their accuracy never better than questionable. They make nice prizes in caramel-covered popcorn, but there are infinitely better choices for wilderness route finding.

Cruiser Compasses

Cruiser compasses are the most accurate you can buy and are also the most expensive of the hand-held compasses. Cruiser compasses are designed for professionals such as timber cruisers, geologists, and survey crews. Prices start at over $100 dollars. If you want a quality instrument and are not concerned with price or weight, then a cruiser compass is your best choice. If, however, you are interested only in direction, expressed in degree readings, the lower-priced lightweight orienteering compass would be more suitable. Probably the best cruiser compasses available today are Brunton's Pocket Transits. Brunton (see Resources for address) has been making very high-quality compasses for professionals since 1894.

The standard cruiser compass is easy to identify because the compass card is numbered counterclockwise. Other stan-

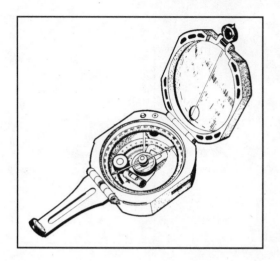

*Cruiser compass
(Brunton Pocket
Transit).*

dard features include an adjustment for magnetic declinations (a screw mechanism that moves the compass card left or right as required) and tick marks for each of the 360 degrees on the compass card. On most models, the needle locks in position when the cover is closed; this cuts down on needle wear over the life of the instrument. Several other features commonly built into cruiser compasses are really of interest only to professionals—for example, scales and bubble levels that determine slope incline and elevation and measure both horizontal and vertical angles. Most cruiser compasses are a little too heavy (8 ounces and up) for people concerned about excess weight, such as backpackers. Brunton has recently introduced a lightweight cruiser compass (about 5 ounces), however, with all of the features of heavier units.

Orienteering Compasses

The orienteering compass has a needle that operates independently of the card. The compass housing, which has 0- to 360-degree readings stamped in a clockwise direction around the

*Orienteering com-
pass.*

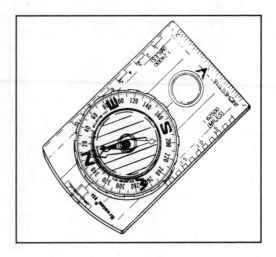

dial, can be turned so that any degree reading is indicated by
the direction-of-travel arrow. The direction-of-travel arrow
itself is permanently stamped into the base.

An orienteering compass is the best type for almost any
kind of travel in the great outdoors. These familiar-looking
compasses are inexpensive, lightweight (less than an ounce),
rugged, and dependable. They have a clear plastic base and a
rotating degree ring, and are commonly filled with a damping
liquid. Orienteering compasses are widely sold in sporting-
goods, backpacking-equipment, and even department stores
throughout the country. At one time all units were made by
the Silva Company, but now several other companies (including Brunton) offer high-quality units as well.

For around $10, you can purchase a good orienteering
compass that has all of the features necessary to navigate in
the wilds. Usually, however, an adjustment for magnetic declination is not one of the features on an orienteering compass.

An orienteering compass is the simplest to use for following a compass bearing. Point the direction-of-travel arrow at

your objective, then turn the compass dial or housing until the needle points to the N symbol (or 0- or 360-degree mark). This is known as orienting the compass to north. The degree reading just above the direction-of-travel arrow is the bearing of the objective. While walking toward the objective, you need only to hold the compass flat and steady, keeping the needle oriented to north; the direction-of-travel arrow will point the way. When you reach this objective, check the compass again and sight to a new objective, with the compass needle oriented to north on the compass housing. Anyone can learn to use an orienteering compass in about twenty minutes. Using this type of compass, you will be surprised at the speed and ease with which you are able to follow a course.

Compass Features

Some features make a compass easier to use or more accurate; others increase the versatility of the instrument. When shopping for a compass, consider only those features that will be an aid to you. For example, a surveyor could use a clinometer, for measuring angles of inclination, on a cruiser compass, but a backpacker or hunter really has no use for this feature. Here are brief descriptions of the most popular—and most useful—features.

Damping. Damping slows down movement of the needle so that it will come to rest more quickly. This saves time when you are taking many readings, such as when following a route. There are three systems for damping a compass needle: induction damping, liquid damping, and needle lock levers.

Induction damping works by magnetic force, dependent on the velocity of the needle. The more the needle swings, the greater the force to dampen the swing. When the needle stops, the magnetic force of the induction damping system also stops, so the damping effect on the compass needle at rest is nil.

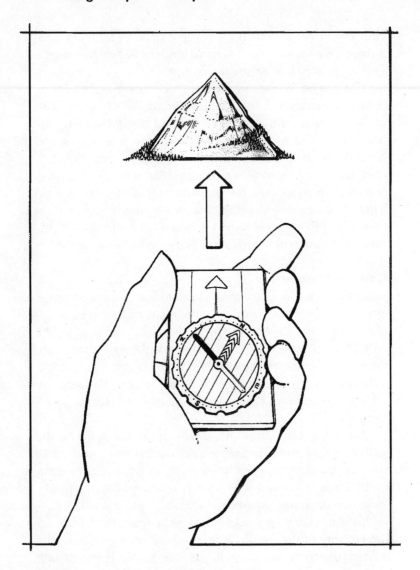

To orient an orienteering compass to north, begin by pointing the direction-of-travel arrow at your objective. Then turn the compass housing until the compass needle is pointing at the N symbol.

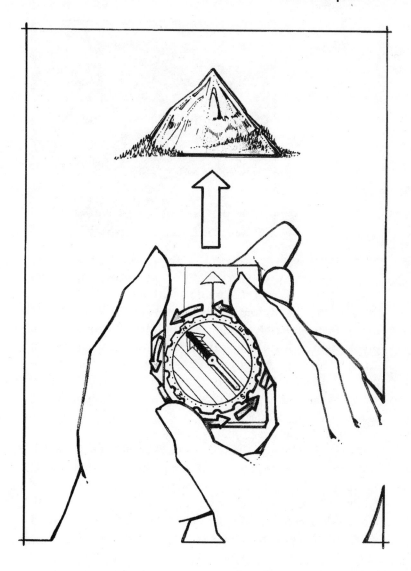

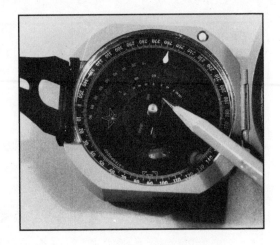

The Brunton Pocket Transit has a built-in induction damping system.

The Brunton Company builds induction damping into its line of Pocket Transits. On models with induction damping, there is a magnet mounted on each side of the compass needle, just above the pivot point. Surrounding the center of the pivot point is a tiny copper cup. As the compass needle swings, the magnets set up their own magnetic field inside the cup and help to quickly bring the needle to rest. When the swing of the compass needle stops, the induction damping magnets no longer affect it.

Liquid damping is probably the most common method of slowing down compass needle movement, and nearly all orienteering compasses are liquid damped. Liquid damping is fast and reliable. The liquid commonly has a freezing point of around -40 degrees F, so for most of us, liquid damping will work well. The case of a liquid-damped compass must be well made to prevent damage that could cause the liquid to drain out of the unit. One problem often encountered with liquid-filled compasses is the appearance of a small air bubble inside the case, especially at high elevations. As a rule, unless the air bubble is larger than 1/4 inch, there is no cause for alarm. If the

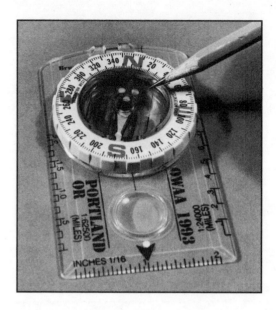

Liquid damping is probably the most common system.

air bubble is much larger or does not disappear at lower elevations, return the compass to the manufacturer for a replacement.

Needle lock levers are the third and by far the most frustrating damping system. Old army lensatic compasses have a needle lift lever that works only when the cover is closed. In fact, the lever is activated by closing the cover. Other compasses have a small pin that is depressed to lift the compass needle off the pivot point. To slow down needle travel, you must alternately press and release the lever until the needle comes to rest. Compasses equipped with only a needle lifter for damping can be a chore to use in the field.

People often have assumed that needle quiver indicates compass accuracy. In truth, needle quiver merely means that the needle has not yet come to rest. It may also indicate that the inside of the needle balance point has been worn by the jeweled needle pivot and therefore cannot come to rest. If a

The compass needle is locked in position when the cover is closed on this old army compass.

compass needle quivers excessively—and it will if not damped in some way—consider buying another compass, as this one will prove quite annoying and will offer questionable accuracy at best.

Sights. Sights are built into many compasses for ease in pinpointing an objective. Any compass that does not have some means of sighting an objective will leave a lot to be desired during use in the field. The main types of sights currently in use are lensatic sights, prismatic sights, V or rifle-type sights, and direction-of-travel-arrow sights.

Lensatic sights are found on old military compasses. A lens, which is part of the rear sight, has a twofold purpose: to magnify the compass dial, so that you can determine a degree reading, and to sight the objective. To use a lensatic sight, you line up the notch on top of the lens housing with a wire on the cover of the compass (the front sight) and the objective. A lensatic compass must be held close to the face for sighting and for reading the compass bearing, which can lead to error, especially if the sights are not perfectly aligned.

Prismatic sights are slow to operate. The objective must be lined up between rear and front sights, and then a degree bearing read through the prism part of the rear sight. Prismatic sights can be very accurate when the alignment of the prism is true. Unfortunately, there is little you can do to determine if these sights are, in fact, true. As with lensatic sights, these work best when held relatively close to your eye. Another drawback is that a prismatic sight is difficult to read in low-light conditions.

V or *rifle-type sights* are offered on several compasses, often in conjunction with a mirrored cover. To use this type, you simply hold the compass at eye level about 12 inches from your face and sight the objective with a V-shaped trough or slot on the compass housing. Once you've lined up the objective in the sight, you read the bearing from the mirror cover, where a line crosses the compass card degree readings. Fairly accurate readings, within 2 degrees, are possible with

Tilt the mirror to see the face of the compass

Sight the object while looking over the tips of the front and rear sights

V or rifle sights are used for determining a bearing.

this type of sighting system, but they are not as quick to use as direction-of-travel-arrow sights.

Direction-of-travel-arrow sights are found on orienteering compasses. The arrow is inscribed in the base of the compass, so it cannot be knocked out of alignment. Orienteering compasses with this type of sight are accurate within 2 degrees at a quick glance (within 1 degree with more care), which is generally sufficient for following a compass bearing. The most attractive feature of direction-of-travel-arrow sights is that they are very fast to use—you simply point the arrow at your objective, orient the housing to north, and read the bearing. You can hold the compass anywhere between your chin and your hip, out about 6 inches from your body.

Needle Lifters. A needle lifter is found on most cruiser compasses. To lift the compass needle off the pivot point when the compass is not in use, a lever is activated when the cover of the compass is closed. Precision surveying instruments should have some means of lifting the compass needle when not in use to prevent wear. On lightweight orienteering compasses, however, a needle lifter is rare. A needle lifter, as mentioned earlier, can also be used to dampen needle movement.

Luminous Dials. A luminous dial is a handy feature when you are traveling in the dark or in low-light conditions. As a rule, you can charge up a luminous dial by shining a flashlight on it for a few moments, and then it will glow for several hours.

Level Indicators. Level indicators use a tiny, round bubble to indicate that the compass is being held flat. Because precise accuracy is dependent, at least in part, on holding a compass level, this feature is important on professional navigating and surveying instruments. Less expensive orienteering compasses will rarely have a level indicator; most users have no problem holding the compass level enough to obtain reasonably accurate readings.

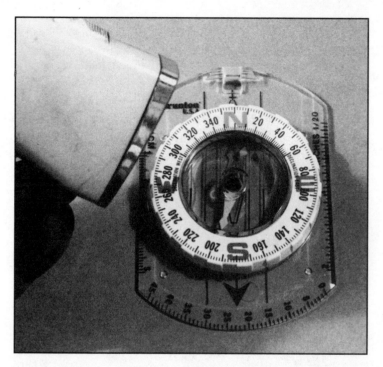

A luminous dial is a handy feature if you ever have to travel in the dark. Simply charge the dial for a few minutes with a flashlight.

Adjustment Features. A magnetic declination adjustment feature is found on all cruiser compasses and most of the expensive orienteering compasses. This feature adds to the cost of the unit, but is well worth the price if you plan to use the compass with a topographical map. In the extreme eastern and western parts of the United States, magnetic declination can be as great as 22 degrees. Travel is much easier if this deviation is taken care of by an adjustment to the compass rather than by a mental calculation at each reading. Although adding or subtracting the magnetic deviation for a particular part of the country is not difficult, there is always a chance that you might forget to perform the necessary calculation. Failing to take a 20-degree magnetic declination into consideration on a 3-mile hike will steer you more than a mile from your objective. Many people feel that a magnetic declination adjustment feature is well worth the added cost.

Magnifying Glasses. A magnifying glass is a common

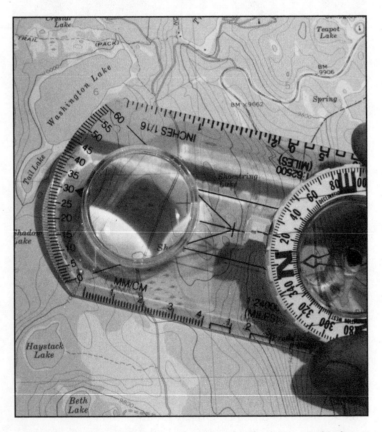

A magnifying glass can help you to better see detail on a topographical map.

addition to orienteering compasses. It is usually mounted in the flat, clear plastic base and is handy for reading detail on topographical maps, especially the larger-scale (15-minute series) maps.

Cases. A compass is useless to you if it is crammed somewhere inside your pack. If your compass is handy, you will use it frequently and become more familiar with its operation. Many compasses come with a special carrying case that can be attached to your belt. If you are backpacking and are using a hip belt, attach the case to your hip belt. An even better way to carry a compass is on a lanyard around your neck. You can tuck the compass into a shirt pocket or allow it to hang when not in use. A compass carried in this manner is always accessible and tough to lose.

CHECKING COMPASS ACCURACY

In most cases, a good compass will work properly for a lifetime. If, however, the accuracy of your compass is ever in doubt, there are several ways to check whether it is pointing to magnetic north.

One way is to compare the direction of north indicated by your compass with Polaris, the North Star or Pole Star. This star has been used by land and sea navigators for centuries. It is one celestial body that remains in a constant position: almost directly over the geographical North Pole. An example will help illustrate how to check your compass against the North Star. Let's say that you are camping in the Big Horn National Forest in Wyoming, around the forty-fifth parallel, where the magnetic declination is 13 degrees east. You have consulted your map to determine both meridian and declination. To check your compass, hold it steady in the palm of your hand or lay it on a solid, flat surface. Note the direction the needle is pointing, then look into the night sky at an angle of about 45 degrees. Polaris should be located about 13

degrees to the left of the direction indicated by your compass.
Another way to check compass accuracy involves a watch

The location of Polaris is at the end of the handle of the Little Dipper and about five times the height of the Big Dipper's cup away.

and the sun. Your watch must have minute and hour hands (digital watches are useless for this check) and must be set for

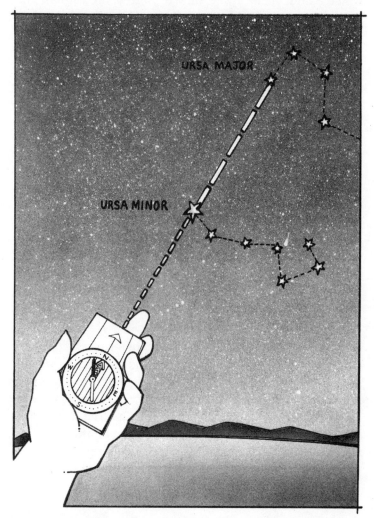

You can use Polaris to check the accuracy of your compass. But first you must know the magnetic declination for your area.

standard time rather than daylight saving time. Also, you must be able to see the sun fairly clearly. First, point the watch's hour hand at the sun. To find south, estimate the halfway point between the 12 and the hour hand (which is still pointing at the sun). True north is in the opposite direction. Simply compare the direction indicated by your watch with a reading from your compass, adding or subtracting magnetic declination if necessary. The readings should be fairly close.

If you don't have a watch, you can use the sun along with a straight stick about 4 feet long. Push the stick into the ground in an open area. The area around the stick must be clear so that you'll be able to see the stick's shadow. Mark the location of the shadow. Wait for the shadow to move a few inches (about fifteen minutes), then mark the new location. Finally, draw a line through the two shadow marks. The line will run east-west, the first mark being the west end of the line. A line perpendicular to this line will run north-south.

You can also use this setup to give you a rough approximation of the time of day. Once you've established an east-west line, draw a line parallel to it with the stick in the middle. The west end of the line represents 6:00 A.M., and the east end 6:00 P.M. Noon is located where the north-south line crosses both sets of lines with the stick in the middle. The distance between 6:00 A.M. and noon represents the morning hours 7:00 to 11:00 A.M., spaced equally. The afternoon hours are on the other side of the north-south line. The shadow cast by the stick will fall on either the morning or afternoon section, and you can estimate the time based on the location of the shadow. Though this setup is rough, you'll be surprised at the closeness to the actual time.

The sun's position is also a rough indicator of direction during the day. The catch is that it usually does not rise and set exactly due east or west, but slightly left or right. In the

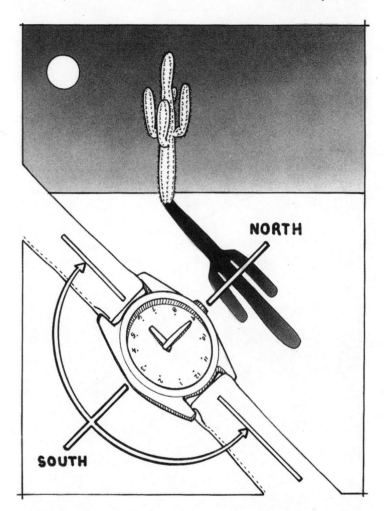

To tell direction with a watch in the Northern Hemisphere, point the hour hand at the sun; south will lie halfway between the hour hand and twelve.

summer, it rises to the left (north) of east and sets to the right (north) of west. In the winter, it rises on the right (south) of east and sets to the left (south) of west. Only on the vernal

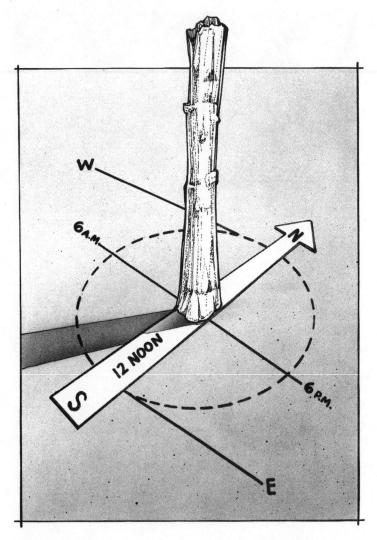

You can use a stick and the sun's shadow to tell you both direction and time.

equinox (March 21) and the autumnal equinox (September 21) does the sun travel due east to due west. In the summer, the sun will travel from the northeast until noon, be overhead at noon, and travel northwest in the afternoon. To determine where the sun will rise the next morning, take a bearing on the direction it sets and subtract 180 degrees.

NAVIGATING WITH COMPASS ONLY

In many cases, a compass can be of tremendous value alone— for example, if you are camping and plan a day hike for exploring, fishing, hunting, photographing, or just plain wandering. Before leaving camp, pick out some objective in the distance, say a mountain peak, and note the compass bearing to it. Later, when you want to return to camp, simply reverse the process and calculate your back bearing—a compass heading in reverse. Determine a back bearing as follows: If the bearing is more than 180 degrees, subtract 180 degrees to determine your back bearing; if the bearing is less than 180 degrees, add 180 degrees. If you headed out at 300 degrees, your back bearing is 120 degrees (300 minus 180).

Whenever you are heading out on a compass bearing and returning on a back bearing, it is imperative that you keep checking your compass to make certain you're on course. This is not always easy to do, because of detours around fallen trees, boulders, swamps, and other natural obstacles. One way to build a safety cushion into your readings is to deliberately follow a course that will put you left or right of your objective.

For example, let's assume that you are camped on a river that flows south, and you plan a day hike to a nearby lake for some fishing. You've been told that this lake lies about 1 mile due east of the camp, so your bearing will be east (90 degrees) to find the lake and west (270 degrees) to return to camp. You easily find the lake after an hour's walk, catch some nice trout, and now are ready to return to camp. Following a back bearing of 270 degrees (90 plus 180) should lead directly back to camp. On the hike in, however, you encountered several natural detours that really prevented a straight route. While it would be easy to find the river on which you are camped, you might not know if you should go upstream or down to find camp. By following a compass bearing of about 290 degrees, you can be sure that when you do finally reach the river, camp will be downstream. Thus, deliberate error can help you find the way back if the objective lies on a river, road, or trail.

Using the back bearing also works well when objectives can be seen for the trips both to and from a given point. This time you are camping on the end of a small lake surrounded by relatively flat forest terrain. In the distance, clearly visible from camp, is a mountain peak on a bearing of 50 degrees. You decide to climb to its summit to see the view from up there. Compass secured around your neck, you head out from camp on a 50-degree compass bearing. Soon the forest is deep, and neither camp nor mountain peak can be seen. Nevertheless, you proceed on a 50-degree bearing and eventually reach the base of the mountain. The view from the top is spectacular—you can see for miles. In fact, you can see the lake.

When it's time to go back to camp, the formula for determining the back bearing yields 230 degrees (50 plus 180). Trying to hit the camp, however, which is on one end of the lake, may result in missing both the lake and the camp. The lake is large enough that you can use it as an objective instead of the camp. Before descending, you take a bearing on the center of the lake: 240 degrees. Armed with this information, you should be able to make it back to camp quite easily; once you reach the lakeshore, you simply walk to the left until you hit camp.

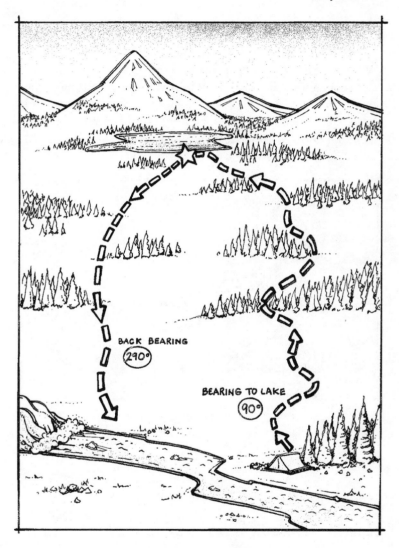

BACK BEARING
290°

BEARING TO LAKE
90°

Deliberate error can be used to your advantage when you are trying to reach a distant line (such as a river, trail, or road) and the terrain does not lend itself to a straight line of travel.

A compass can also help you set up a more comfortable camp. If your camp faces east, the first warming rays of sun will take the chill off the camp while various morning chores are done. This is especially handy when snow-camping in the winter or at high elevations in the summer, where nights tend to be cold. If you plan to sleep late, as on a rest day, or are camping in hot weather, locate camp on the west side of a hill or facing west to avoid the early warming rays of the sun.

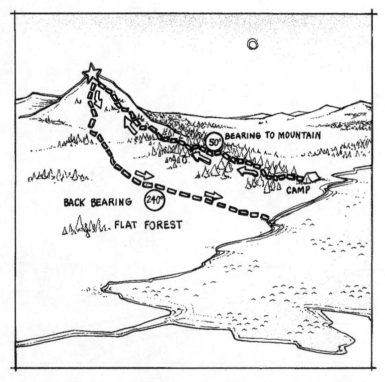

Return by a back bearing of 240 degrees, rather than a true back bearing of 230 degrees. Then when you reach the lake, you know to simply turn left and follow the shoreline back to camp. Traveling in this manner builds some margin for error into your plan, and you can be certain of reaching your objective.

• TWO •

Understanding Maps

For every type of travel and destination, a map has been designed to make the trip easier, faster, and if you know how

You can find a map for almost any place you want to travel.

to read the map, more interesting. There are very few places left in this world that haven't been mapped.

Presently more than five hundred types of maps are produced annually by governmental agencies alone, including topographical maps, orthophoto maps, population density maps, soil maps, water district maps, coastal waterway maps, national and state park maps, airline route maps, moon maps, and star maps. Add to this list road maps, maps drawn by outdoor writers—fishing maps, hunting maps, treasure maps—and those produced by gasoline companies, tire companies, resorts, and equipment manufacturers. The trick is to pick the right kind of map for your specific needs.

ROAD MAPS

Chances are that you already have more map-reading ability than you think. Big-city residents and visitors are accustomed to decoding public-transportation systems with maps. Shopping malls have fancy display directories. And almost everyone has spent enough hours navigating on automobile trips to be familiar with the most common of all maps: road maps.

Road maps are designed to be simple to read. A grid format is used to help you locate specific points. Each column is numbered, and each row is named with a letter. The location of any place on the map can thus be described with a number and letter.

To find a town or point of interest on a road map, first look it up in the index and find its number and letter designations. Then simply find the appropriate column and follow it until it intersects with the row given. Some destinations that are on the map may not be listed in the index; thus it's helpful to know the names of nearby cities or towns. Once you've located your destination, note the intersecting highways and roads to plan the best route.

Road maps can help you in planning a trip by showing

Road maps are more than handy for finding your way—they are essential.

the travel time to the general area as well. A vacation of three to five days allows about one day of road time.

Even if you've traveled to a destination in the past, it always makes good sense to check a current road map. New roads are always being built, and it may very well be that there's now a newer or faster way to an old favorite place.

Time was when gas stations gave away road maps. Now, if you can even find a gas station that has maps, they cost a few dollars apiece. Automobile clubs provide free maps and current traveling information to members. Consult your local telephone directory for a club in your area.

A road atlas can be handy when planning a trip. A current one will show not only old and new roads, but also those under construction. The larger road atlases usually show some details such as campgrounds and points of interest. There also are books of maps designed just for road campers.

SPECIAL-INTEREST MAPS

Special-interest maps can help you get what you want from a wilderness trip. Hundreds of maps are designed specifically for hikers, fishermen, hunters, canoeists, and other outdoorsmen. These special maps, including fishing maps, trail maps (for hikers, cross-country skiers, snowmobilers, horsemen), and maps of scenic points of interest, can provide valuable information. Cross-checking several maps will give you a fuller picture of a park or wilderness area. You may discover, for example, that trails marked on the winter map for cross-country skiing or snowmobiling are empty during the summer hiking season.

A road atlas is a good trip-planning aid.

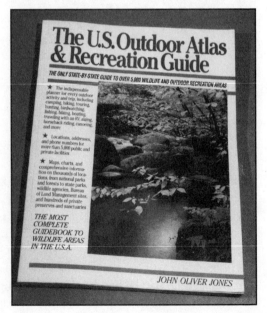

The U.S. Outdoor Atlas & Recreation Guide

THE ONLY STATE-BY-STATE GUIDE TO OVER 5,000 WILDLIFE AND OUTDOOR RECREATION AREAS

★ The indispensable planner for every outdoor activity and trip, including camping, hiking, touring, hunting, birdwatching, fishing, biking, boating, traveling with an RV, skiing, horseback riding, canoeing, and more.

★ Locations, addresses, and phone numbers for more than 5,000 public and private facilities.

★ Maps, charts, and comprehensive information on thousands of locations, from national parks and forests to state parks, wildlife agencies, Bureau of Land Management sites, and hundreds of private preserves and sanctuaries.

THE MOST COMPLETE GUIDEBOOK TO WILDLIFE AREAS IN THE U.S.A.

JOHN OLIVER JONES

Very specific maps can be invaluable if your wilderness goal is very defined. For example, the National Park Service has found that most visitors to Arches National Park in Utah are interested in seeing only those arches that can be reached by automobile. Therefore, for a fee, a road map is available at the park entrance that shows just these arches. Anyone wanting to see more arches—and there are plenty—can check the map in the ranger station or get an Arches National Park topographical map from the United States Geological Survey (USGS).

As a rule, the best sources for special-interest maps are the federal and state agencies that oversee particular wilder-

Special-interest maps are available from many sources and can provide you with a wealth of information about specific areas.

ness areas. Their names and addresses are listed in the Resources. When writing, allow time for your request to be processed.

Every state has a fish and game or environmental protection agency, which publishes maps of recreational areas in that state. State park maps not only give a general picture of an area, but also list regulations for such things as fishing, hunting, boating, and aircraft.

Federal agencies that supply information and maps include the U.S. Forest Service (part of the U.S. Department of Agriculture), which controls 187 million acres designated as the National Forest System; the National Park Service which oversees 285 natural, historical, and recreational areas of national significance; and the Bureau of Land Management, (BLM), which controls 457 million acres in twelve western states. The BLM oversees about 60 percent of all public lands in the United States, mostly desert and mountain areas. Although the BLM doesn't offer nearly as much information and maps as the other federal agencies, it may be worth writing to the regional office for the area where you're planning a trip.

Special maps and guides are also available from clubs and book publishers. The Adirondack Mountain Club publishes a guide to trails in those mountains. The Sierra Club also has a series of very helpful travel guides, including *Adventuring in the Rockies*. Other books, such as *Starr's Guide to the John Muir Trail* and the *High Sierra Region*, can also be found in bookstores.

Probably the best sources of new information about wilderness trips are magazine articles. Magazines such as *Field & Stream*, *Outdoor Life*, *Sports Afield*, *Western Outdoors*, *Backpacker*, and *Outside* are full of current travel information. Articles about specific trips, are full of tips and often include maps.

TOPOGRAPHICAL MAPS

Road maps will get you to a wilderness area and special-interest maps will help you plan your trip, but the most basic and important wilderness travel map is the topographical map. Topos are very detailed maps that show land features, water, elevation, forests, roads, trails, and man-made structures.

Most outdoorsmen have probably seen a topographical map, as one is commonly posted at ranger stations and national forest trailheads. It is surprising, however, that most people who travel in wild places don't know the language of these maps and thus miss a lot of important information.

A first encounter with a topo can be confusing. Its symbolism and three-dimensional representation are an unfamiliar way of viewing the world. Some areas are green, some blue, some simply white. Red and brown lines seem to be everywhere, some close together and others farther apart. All

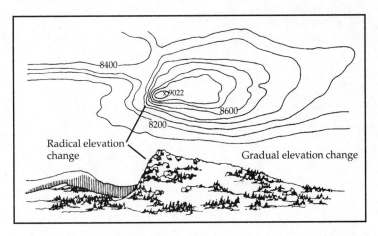

An actual piece of land (above) and how it is represented on a topographical map (below).

of these colors, lines, and symbols have important meanings. Once you learn the language of these maps, it's relatively easy to learn about an area before you actually go there.

Various colors on a topographical map represent types of terrain. Green areas denote vegetation, most commonly forest or brush. Blue areas and blue lines indicate water: Circles or irregular shapes are ponds or small lakes; small dashed or squiggly blue lines are streams; broader lines are rivers. White areas mean that there's very little vegetation—a desert or rocky alpine area.

The red lines forming perfect squares across the face of any topographical map are called *section lines*. In the center of each of these squares is a section number from 1 to 36. Most of the United States, with the exception of the original thirteen colonies, is broken down into squares, 6 miles on a side, called

6	5	4	3	2	1
7	8	9	10	11	12
18	17	16	15	14	13
19	20	21	22	23	24
30	29	28	27	26	25
31	32	33	34	35	36

Township sections measure 1 square mile and are numbered as shown.

townships. Each township contains 36 sections. The township sections are 1 square mile each and are numbered as in the illustration.

Brown lines on a topographical map are important and indicate contour interval and elevation of the landscape. The space between any two of these lines represents an increase or decrease in elevation that varies from one map to another. In the mountains, the intervals shown on the map could be 40 to 80 feet; on flat terrain they might be 20 feet. The closer together the contour lines, the steeper the terrain. The elevation number is written only beside the darker contour lines, known as *index contour lines*. Contour interval is indicated in the bottom margin.

Topographical maps use many different symbols to represent man-made structures and roads. In most cases, these symbols resemble the object denoted. For example, a tiny black square is a dwelling, a black square with a cross on top is a church, and one with a flag is a school.

A topographical map is oriented along true north and south meridians. The left and right margins, therefore, point to true north and south. The longitudinal and latitudinal lines are denoted by numbers in the map margins. The longitude and latitude numbers indicate which part of the world the map represents. Latitudinal lines give the distance from the Equator, and longitudinal lines distance from the Prime Meridian, a line running from the geographical North Pole through Greenwich, England, to the South Pole.

Topographical map margins contain a wealth of useful information, including the date the map was printed and last field-checked, the map's scale, a scale ruler, the contour interval spacing, names of adjoining maps, and magnetic declination information. To learn the locations of these pieces of information, examine an actual topographical map or the illustration of a topo border given here. Although there may

Some common topographical map symbols.

be some variations in older maps, these elements are always found in the margin area around any topographical map.

In the top right corner are the name of the map, the state, and the series (7½-minute series or 15-minute series, for example). The maps are generally named after a prominent feature, such as a high peak or river, or a township. In this corner and all others are the names of adjoining maps. Consult these other maps as necessary for planning your trip.

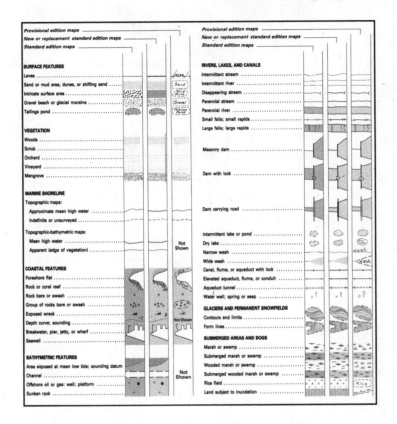

In the bottom right corner, the name of the map is repeated. Also given here are the longitude and latitude designations, the last time this map was field-checked, the series, and usually road classifications (such as light duty, jeep trail, or pack trail).

Moving to the left along the bottom margin is an outline map of the state; within this outline map, a black box marks the location of the particular topo.

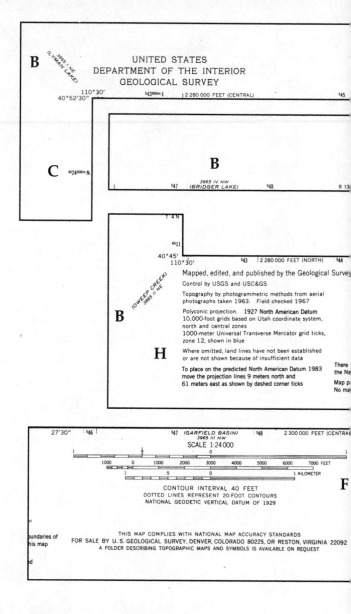

B

(LYMAN LAKE)
3965 I NE

UNITED STATES
DEPARTMENT OF THE INTERIOR
GEOLOGICAL SURVEY

110°30'
40°52'30"

543000m E   2 280 000 FEET (CENTRAL)

545

C   4524000m N.

B

3965 IV NW
(BRIDGER LAKE)

547   548   R 13

T 4 N

4511

40°45'
110°30'

543   2 280 000 FEET (NORTH)   544

(OWEEP CREEK)
3965 II NE

B

H

Mapped, edited, and published by the Geological Survey

Control by USGS and USC&GS

Topography by photogrammetric methods from aerial
photographs taken 1963.   Field checked 1967

Polyconic projection.   1927 North American Datum
10,000-foot grids based on Utah coordinate system,
north and central zones
1000-meter Universal Transverse Mercator grid ticks,
zone 12, shown in blue

Where omitted, land lines have not been established
or are not shown because of insufficient data

To place on the predicted North American Datum 1983
move the projection lines 9 meters north and
61 meters east as shown by dashed corner ticks

There
the Na

Map p
No ma

27'30"   546   547   (GARFIELD BASIN)   548   2 300 000 FEET (CENTRAL
3965 III NW
SCALE 1:24 000

0

1000   0   1000   2000   3000   4000   5000   6000   7000 FEET

1   5   0   1 KILOMETER

F

CONTOUR INTERVAL 40 FEET
DOTTED LINES REPRESENT 20-FOOT CONTOURS
NATIONAL GEODETIC VERTICAL DATUM OF 1929

oundaries of
his map

THIS MAP COMPLIES WITH NATIONAL MAP ACCURACY STANDARDS
FOR SALE BY U. S. GEOLOGICAL SURVEY, DENVER, COLORADO 80225, OR RESTON, VIRGINIA 22092
A FOLDER DESCRIBING TOPOGRAPHIC MAPS AND SYMBOLS IS AVAILABLE ON REQUEST

d

The information contained on all USGS maps is shown on the map margin pieces
above. A. The name of the map, the state, and the series. B. Names of adjoining
maps. C. Meridian lines (left and right margin). D. Longitude lines (top and bot-

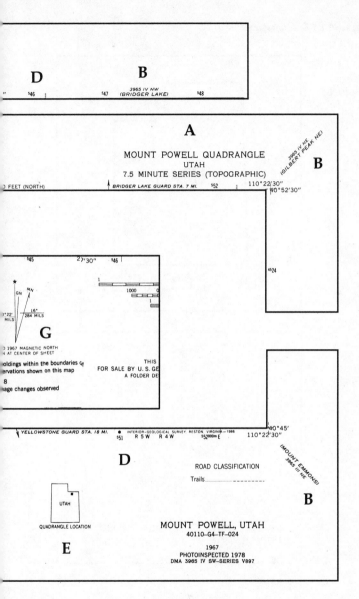

D

B

3965 IV NW
(BRIDGER LAKE)

⁵46   ⁵47   ⁵48

A

MOUNT POWELL QUADRANGLE
UTAH
7.5 MINUTE SERIES (TOPOGRAPHIC)

3965 IV NE
(GILBERT PEAK NE)

B

0 FEET (NORTH)   ↑ BRIDGER LAKE GUARD STA. 7 MI.   ⁵52   110°22′30″
40°52′30″

⁴524

⁵45   2′′30″   ⁵46

1
1000   0
1

GN   MN

0°22′   16°
MILS   284 MILS

G

0 1967 MAGNETIC NORTH
N AT CENTER OF SHEET

oldings within the boundaries of
ervations shown on this map

8
nage changes observed

THIS
FOR SALE BY U. S. GE
A FOLDER DE

↑ YELLOWSTONE GUARD STA. 18 MI.   ● INTERIOR-GEOLOGICAL SURVEY, RESTON, VIRGINIA—1986   40°45′
110°22′30″

⁵51   R 5 W   R 4 W   ⁵52000m E

D

(MOUNT EMMONS)
3965 III NE

ROAD CLASSIFICATION

Trails.................   _ _ _ _ _ _ _

B

UTAH

QUADRANGLE LOCATION

E

MOUNT POWELL, UTAH
40110–G4–TF–024

1967
PHOTOINSPECTED 1978
DMA 3965 IV SW–SERIES V897

tom margin). E. Location of map in state. F. Scale of the map and contour interval.
G. True north orientation and magnetic declination symbol. H. Other information
about the map, such as which agency did the mapping.

The black box
inside the outline
of the state is the
area covered by a
given map.

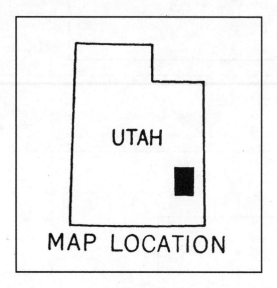

True north and
magnetic north
symbol for a topo
map.

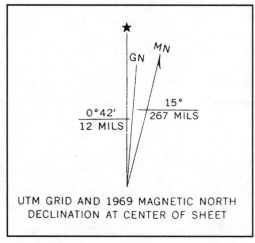

In the bottom center is the scale of the map, both in fig-
ures and on a ruler. Below the scale is the contour interval
(expressed in feet) for the map.

Next is the magnetic declination symbol, showing the directions of grid north (GN), true or geographical north (a star), and magnetic north (MN). Grid north, the direction that the vertical grid lines actually run, is usually different from both true north and magnetic north. Grid north is used by map makers and has no real value to the outdoorsman. Magnetic north, true north, and the magnetic declination between them are what's important.

In the lower left corner is a block of information that includes the name of the agency that did the major work on the map—United States Geological Survey, Department of the Interior, War Department (often the case with older maps), or another federal agency—and the date when the map was last field-checked. Other information in this section is of varying importance, depending on whether you're a hiker, geologist, mapmaker, forester, or whatever. Always read this block of text, as it may contain important information. For example, it will tell you the last time this area was photographed from the air and the agency that did the aerial photography. There also may be a key to fences or boundaries of an Indian reservation or a state park, or you may learn that at the time this map was last updated, there was insufficient information to indicate boundary or fence lines. In the latter case, you may come up against a fence that was not indicated on your map. The text may tell you that unchecked elevations are shown in brown, indicating that the elevations of some of the peaks on the map have not been checked. In most cases, brown elevation numbers are very close to actual elevations (which are always shown in black), so for your purposes they can be relied on.

In the top left corner of the map is repeated the name of the government agency that did most of the work on this map.

When planning a wilderness trip, try to get your hands on 7½-minute-series topographical maps as soon as possible

A state index is handy for helping you decide which topographical maps you will need. State index maps are free from the USGS.

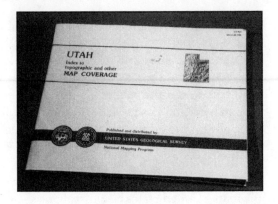

so that you can look over the area. To find out which maps you'll need, consult a state topographical index map. You can buy topo maps at a state office of the USGS, which usually stocks all maps for the state, a map store, or a sporting-goods store. It usually takes several weeks to receive maps by writing to one of the major USGS map centers, located in Virginia and Colorado (see the Resources). It's a good idea to keep a state index map handy for trip planning; purchase points for the topo maps are listed on the state index map.

Even if you've bought maps of the area in past years, updated versions may now be available. Relying on that old map, you may be disappointed to find that a four-wheel-drive trail now passes right by your favorite lake. Many topographical maps are updated annually, but many more are not. For this reason, local and special-purpose maps can also be of help, as they commonly show new roads, trails, shelters, and other developments.

Studying a topo is an important part of pretrip planning. Becoming familiar with an area will help you get the most from your wilderness trip. A topo can make any trip more comfortable and more interesting, and it can rightly be considered a piece of safety gear. In an emergency, it may be critical to know that a spring lies in section 12 or that there is a cabin in section 9. You can jot notes on the back of the map for quick future reference.

Plan your route to take advantage of terrain. Thirty pounds on your back can become a burden after a few hours of hiking, even on a well-beaten trail, and when you strike off cross-country, that same pack load can feel like twice as much. Choose compass headings that will allow you to avoid as much climbing as possible. Avoid areas where contour interval lines on the map are close together, as this indicates steep ground. The most direct route may happen to be straight up a 60-foot rock face, in which case it's better to take a longer route around.

If there is no way that you'll be able to avoid a difficult piece of terrain, at least you can be prepared. For example, you can add a rope to your basic equipment so that you can haul gear up a steep rock face after you've climbed it. If you'll have to cross a river, carry an air mattress instead of a foam pad so that you can float your gear—and you'll still have a comfortable bed at night.

Take advantage of any natural and man-made navigational aids. Jeep, horse, or foot trails shown on the topo can be your route into or out of an area. If a stream flows through several lakes, it can lead you from one to the next.

Plan your route to take advantage of streams, ponds, and lakes. Keep in mind that on a typical summer day, a hiker should drink at least 1 gallon of water. Know in advance where you can find water when you need it, and be sure to take along water filtration and purification gear and purify all water before you drink it. Water—drinkable, fishable, clear, cool, and moving— is rarely in short supply in true wilderness areas. Bodies of water also make good checkpoints.

Topographical map symbols have many navigational uses. During the planning stages, they might clue you in to

Become familiar with an area by studying topos before you begin your trip.

good places to cross a river or places to avoid, such as a rapids or a waterfall. Swamp symbols will tip you off to another area to avoid. In the field, map symbols can help you orient the map or serve as checkpoints on your progress. A glance at the map and a hiker can say, "We'll take a rest stop when we reach that cabin, about two miles down the trail in section eleven."

The USGS draws topographical maps in several different scales. On a 1:24,000-scale map, 1 inch equals 24,000 inches (or 2,000 feet) on the ground. The 1:24,000-scale map, or $7\frac{1}{2}$-minute quadrangle map, is the most popular with outdoorsmen and is the backbone of the national topographic program. A map of this scale covers a four-sided, almost rectangular area bounded by $7\frac{1}{2}$ minutes of longitude and $7\frac{1}{2}$ minutes of latitude. Because longitude lines converge, the actual area covered ranges from about 70 square miles in the Deep South to about 50 square miles along the Canadian border.

On a 1:62,500-scale or 15-minute-series topographical map, 1 inch on the map equals almost 1 mile on the ground (5,280 feet). This map covers roughly 197 to 282 square miles, again depending on the location.

In some sections of the United States, 15-minute-series topographical maps are still available, but they are gradually being replaced by $7\frac{1}{2}$-minute-series topos, as their greater detail is an aid to geologic explorers and prospectors. Nevertheless, a 15-minute series map can be very handy for a trip covering a lot of country, such as a canoe trip or an extended backpacking trip.

On a 1:250,000 scale map, 1 inch equals about 4 miles on the ground. These maps are used mainly for regional planning and topographical bases for other types of maps. Each map in this series covers from 4,580 to 8,669 square miles.

On a 1:500,000-scale map, 1 inch on the map equals about 8 miles on the ground. This scale is most commonly used for state maps. They cover large areas—28,174 to 30,462 square mile—and are used for planning by state governments, as they give a total picture of a state. They can also help outdoorsmen zero in on large roadless areas.

The scale of 1:1,000,000, where 1 inch equals about 16 miles on the ground, is used for the International Map of the World. This map can be handy for broad geographical studies, even though the names of some countries change from time to time.

NAVIGATING WITH MAP ONLY

On many occasions, a topographical map will be the only navigational tool needed. The most accurate means for the wilderness traveler—and the only way to truly bushwhack—is with both map and compass, but that method is not necessary if your route follows blazed trails. With just the topo, you are left free to observe wildlife, plants, scenery, and just generally enjoy the trip.

Following a marked trail through a wilderness area is quite simple, and its advantages should not be overlooked. In some parts of the country—along the Appalachian Trail in the East, for example—all main trails are marked with metal disks nailed to trees along the route at about eye level. These metal disks are painted a solid color that indicates the particular trail you are following. The trail name or designation is often printed on each marker; in this case, it is very easy to identify the trail if you can find a marker. Trail markers are nailed to both sides of a tree so that they can be seen coming and going, and are spaced about fifty yards apart.

In the West, trails are generally marked in a different manner. More often than not, these trails are marked with an ax blaze cut into the bark of trees along the route. It's common to find a splash of white paint in some national forest trail systems as well. On heavily used western trails—national forest trails, for example—you'll usually find signs at trailheads and junctions that give distances to various objectives, such as a large lake or mountain summit.

On many marked trail systems, you almost don't have to

look for trail markers; just follow the well-beaten path. This is especially true when pack animals are commonly used on the trails. The farther you get into the backcountry, however, the less trodden the path and the more valuable the trail markers or ax blazes.

In desert areas, where trees are not available, piles of rocks, called *cairns* or *ducks*, are the most common means of marking trails. These markers are usually easy to follow because the piles of stone look unnatural and are easy to spot.

On the trail, a quick glance at the topo will reveal how much distance you've traveled: the name of that lake, or pond, or mountain off in the distance; and the best place for your next rest stop. Where trails intersect, the map shows where the new trail came from and where it goes. When I stop for a rest, the first thing I do is to pull out the topo map—not because I'm afraid of getting lost, but because I'm naturally curious. How far is it to Spruce Lake, and how difficult will the trail ahead be compared with the terrain I've covered so far? How high is that peak in the distance? What elevation have I reached?

Working with a map on a marked trail will familiarize you with how the actual terrain looks in relation to a topographical map. This skill can be developed only through actual practice, and it can be developed surprisingly fast by traveling with map close at hand. On later trips that lead through true wilderness on unmarked trails, you'll be better equipped to plan and follow your own route if you have a firm grasp of map-reading skills.

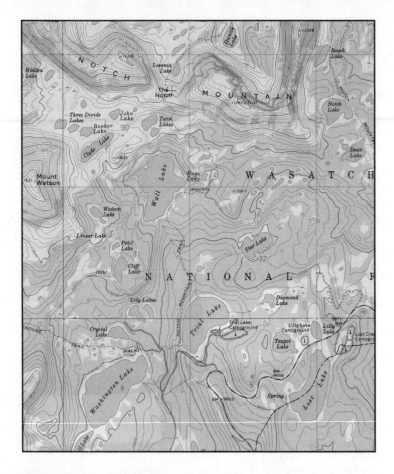

Answer the following questions regarding this section of topographical map. The contour interval is 40 feet.

1. What is the major road type on this map?
2. What sections have campgrounds?
3. What section is the spring in?
4. What section has an unimproved road?
5. What sections have intermittent streams?
6. What is the elevation of Star Lake?
7. What section has the most marsh and swamp areas?
8. Approximately how many square miles does this map cover?
9. Which lake is the spring near?
10. Where are the only buildings on the map?

Answers

1. *Trail.*
2. *Sections 4 and 5.*
3. *Section 5.*
4. *Section 33.*
5. *Sections 30, 31, and 32.*
6. *10,000 feet.*
7. *Section 32.*
8. *Approximately 10 square miles; each section is 1 square mile.*
9. *Lost Lake.*
10. *On the south shore of Trial Lake.*

THREE

Magnetic Declination Demystified

We live in a world with two norths: true north and magnetic north. The difference between the two is called magnetic declination and is an important consideration when a map and compass are used together. A compass always points to magnetic north, whereas all topographical maps are oriented to true north (the North Pole, if you will). Many outdoor travelers ignore magnetic declination and therefore do not navigate precisely. In certain parts of the United States, if you fail to take magnetic declination into consideration, you may never reach your objective.

True north, or the North Pole, is the geographical top of the earth, the spot Robert E. Peary sought and found in 1909. This is also the point through which all longitudinal lines pass. All USGS topographical maps are oriented to true north because the location of the North Pole remains constant.

Magnetic north, the area to which all compass needles point, is less precise in location. Magnetic north is located about 1,300 miles south of true north, presently in northern Canada, northwest of Hudson Bay. The location of magnetic north moves slightly west each year. For example, in the 1950s

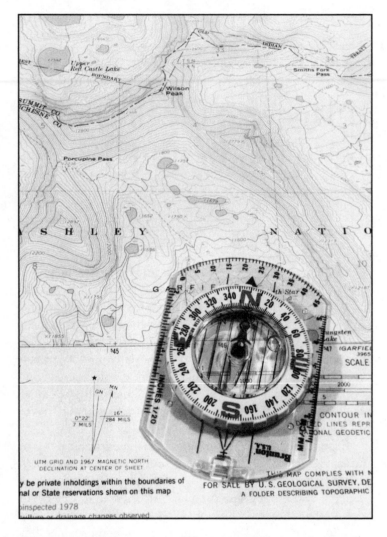

A compass points to magnetic north, but a topographical map is oriented to true north. This difference is called magnetic declination, and adjustment must be made to the compass or map before the two can be used together in the field.

the magnetic declination for Seattle, Washington, was about 23 degrees, but it's now about 22 degrees.

The most accepted theory for the annual westward change is that the force of magnetic north is created by the action of the earth's liquid center. As the earth rotates east on its axis, friction between the liquid core and the relatively solid crust may cause the center to turn just a bit more slowly. This would result in a slight slipping each year.

Since the annual westward change is, in most areas, only a few minutes of longitude a year, there will not be a significant change in any one year or even over a span of several years. Since most compasses carried by nonprofessionals are capable of adjustments of only one 1 degree or more, there would really be little point in knowing that a map has changed 30 minutes. Degrees are important, but for our purposes, minutes are not. Over a ten-year period, however, there may be as much as a 1-degree shift. On the bottom of all topographical maps, the USGS notes the date its magnetic declination was last checked—usually the same date the map was last field-checked.

An isogonic chart illustrates the lines of magnetic declination for the United States. This chart is fairly accurate for ten years. If you want a chart more current than the 1985 version duplicated here, write to the U.S. Department of Commerce, Coast and Geodetic Survey, Distribution Division C44, Washington, DC 20235, and ask for the Isogonic Chart of the United States, Publication #3077.

In the chart, a dark line runs from the west coast of Florida through the Great Lakes. This is the agonic line, an imaginary line passing through both magnetic north and true north. Magnetic declination adjustments are not required along this line. In the western part of North America, magnetic declination is to the east of north; in the eastern part,

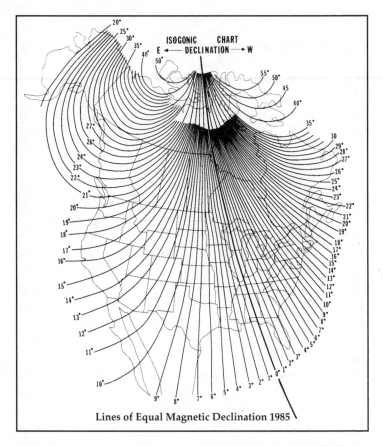

An isogonic chart shows magnetic declination lines for the United States.

magnetic declination is to the west of north. Magnetic declination is most significant on the northeast and northwest coasts. At the bottom of all topographical maps is a magnetic declination symbol showing the directions of true north and magnetic north, and a degree-of-declination figure.

The error that is caused by not adjusting for magnetic declination is equal to the distance traveled (D) times the

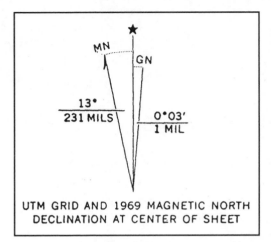

A true north-magnetic north symbol appears on every topographical map.

degree of error (DE) times 1/60. To illustrate, if you walk 3 miles (15,840 feet) toward a lake in an area where the magnetic declination is 10 degrees without adjusting your map or compass, you will miss the lake by 2,640 feet, or a half mile (15,840 times 10 times 1/60).

This built-in error need not plague every effort to navigate with a map and compass. Simple steps allow these adjustments to be made without turning a wilderness trip into a short course in algebra.

ADJUSTING THE COMPASS READING

The basic rule for adjusting a compass reading is this: When east of the agonic line, add degrees of declination to obtain a true north bearing; when west of the agonic line, subtract the number of declination degrees. The magnetic declination deviation can be found in the bottom margin of any USGS topographical map.

All cruiser and most high-tech orienteering compasses can be adjusted for magnetic declination. As a rule, dials on

*Magnetic declina-
tion for the west-
ern (top) and
eastern (bottom)
United States.*

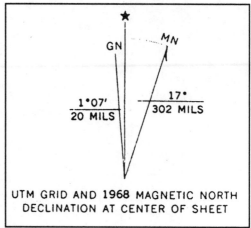

UTM GRID AND 1968 MAGNETIC NORTH
DECLINATION AT CENTER OF SHEET

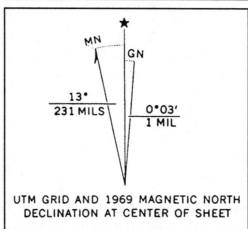

UTM GRID AND 1969 MAGNETIC NORTH
DECLINATION AT CENTER OF SHEET

these specialized compasses are rotated the required number of
degrees of declination so that the compass needle will point to
true north rather than magnetic north. This feature eliminates
the need for any other adjustments to either compass or map.

Most compasses in general use do not have a magnetic
declination adjustment, but you still must take this deviation

Cruiser compasses can be adjusted for magnetic declination and then used with topographical maps with no further adjustment.

into consideration to navigate with any degree of accuracy. To do so, you can simply add or subtract the amount of magnetic declination to every compass heading.

East of the agonic line, add degrees of declination. Let's say you're hiking in the Adirondack Mountains in upstate New York. The magnetic declination is listed as 13 degrees west of north, and the topographical map you're using shows that your objective is on a compass bearing of 250 degrees. Thus, to find your objective, you must follow a compass bearing of 263 degrees (250 plus 13).

West of the agonic line, subtract degrees of declination to find true north. If, for example, you are in the Wind River mountain range in Wyoming, where magnetic declination is 14 degrees east of north, and your objective is on a heading of 280 degrees, you must follow a compass bearing of 266 degrees (280 minus 14).

The only real problem with this method is remembering to do this computation each time you determine a compass course. Forget even once, and you may never reach your objective. One trick to jog your memory is to attach a piece of tape, marked with the magnetic declination for the area, to the back of your compass.

You can place a piece of tape, with the magnetic declination degree reading, on your compass to help you remember the adjustment. You must make an adjustment for every bearing when using this method.

ADJUSTING THE MAP

If your compass does not have an adjustable dial, it is much easier and more dependable to reorient the map to magnetic north than to go through repeated compass calculations. To do so, draw lines across the face of the map in the direction of the magnetic declination. Then it will be a simple matter in the field to orient your map to magnetic north, rather than true north, with the aid of your compass. No further calculations will be necessary.

This method is almost foolproof. There is one caution, however: Check the original orientation of the map before making any adjustments. Although most topos will be drawn

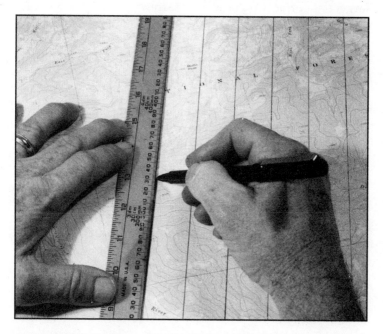

Draw magnetic north lines across the face of a topographical map so that you can use a compass with the map.

to true north, occasionally, especially in very old maps, the magnetic declination line or degree of deviation may be off by 1 or more degrees. If a line drawn between a top and bottom meridian mark appears parallel to the left or right margin, then the map has been drawn to true north.

When you draw lines across the face of your topographical map, space them about 2 inches apart and run them across the entire map. It is very important to draw the lines carefully and accurately. Use a straightedge to help you to draw straight, clean lines. A steel yardstick is good, as it will not bend and is long enough to reach across the entire map. If your straightedge is about 2 inches wide, you can easily judge the spacing between the lines and keep it uniform. Work on a large, flat surface so that you can draw all the lines without repositioning the map. A large kitchen countertop is an ideal working surface.

Always use waterproof ink. Maps have a way of getting wet in the field, and other types of ink will bleed and may mask important map features. A fine-point, felt-tip pen is ideal, because the lines will not hide anything on the map face.

There are three methods for drawing orientation lines on a topographical map. The first, the protractor method, can be used only when the left and right margins on the map are oriented to true north. Determine the magnetic declination for the map by checking the magnetic declination symbol at the bottom of the map. Next, lay a standard protractor in the bottom left corner for western maps or the bottom right corner for eastern maps. You must lay the protractor so that the 0-degree reading aligns with the left (for western maps) or right (for eastern maps) vertical margin of the map, the 90-degree reading aligns with the bottom horizontal margin, and the bottom corner of the map forms the third angle of a right triangle. Now place a mark at the degree of declination for this particular map. Work from the vertical margin, and count over until you reach the proper mark. Then remove the pro-

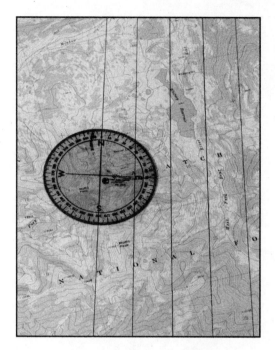

You can use a protractor to help you draw magnetic declination lines on the face of your topographical map.

tractor, and with a ruler and suitable marker, draw a line from the bottom corner of the map to the mark. This is your first magnetic declination line.

Another approach is to extend the magnetic north line in the declination symbol across the face of the map. Drawbacks to this method are that the symbol's small size may make it difficult to accurately extend the line, and near the agonic line, the angle in the symbol is sometimes exaggerated because the actual declination is too small to perceive. If the angle is small, it's best to use the protractor method.

If you have a standard orienteering compass with an adjustable dial and a clear, rectangular base plate, you can use the margin lines of the map and the compass to draw the magnetic declination lines. First, set the compass dial for the map's degree of declination. Place the compass on the map,

You can extend the magnetic north symbol to indicate magnetic declination lines on the face of your topographical map.

and align the lines inside the compass dial with the margin line. Draw a line using the base edge as a ruler. Then extend that line with a ruler and add other parallel lines.

Whichever method you use, the work must be done very carefully. Make certain that the lines run in the right direction. As a general rule of thumb, topographical maps for the western part of the country will have lines running from bottom left to top right, and for the eastern, from bottom right to top left. If the declination for a map is 15 degrees east of north and the lines are drawn 15 degrees west of north, the map will be oriented 30 degrees in the wrong direction. You can double-check

You can also use an orienteering compass to help you draw magnetic declination lines on the face of your topographical map.

before you begin drawing the lines by noting the direction of the magnetic declination symbol at the bottom of the map.

Magnetic declination really poses no problem if you understand the underlying principles. Always remember, when using a topo and compass, to take the difference between true north and magnetic north into consideration and make adjustments to either your compass or your map. Then you'll be able to proceed with the confidence that is the mark of a true outdoorsman.

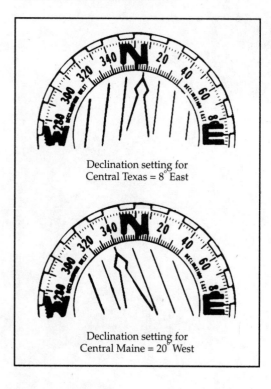

Declination setting for
Central Texas = 8° East

Declination setting for
Central Maine = 20° West

Declination for central Texas is 8 degrees east (top). Declination for central Maine is 20 degrees west (bottom).

· FOUR ·

Navigating with Compass and Map

Once you step off marked trails into true wilderness, you should use topographical maps in conjunction with an orienteering compass for navigation. You should have an orienteering compass with north-pointing lines inside the face of its housing and a topographical map on which you have marked magnetic north lines.

The basics of map and compass use consist of orienting the map, locating your present position, determining the bearing to your objective, and staying on course to that objective. Every bushwhacker should make these tasks second nature and should have a number of tricks for coping with nature's obstacles and irregularities as well.

When you want to determine your azimuth or bearing—your course of travel—first lay the map and compass on a flat surface. Rotate the map until the magnetic north lines you've drawn point in the same direction as the compass needle. The map will then be oriented to magnetic north. Then observe the surrounding countryside to determine your present position on the map. You can determine your location by resection, by line position, with an altimeter, or if there are no landmarks, by using secondary objectives.

A topographical map and a good compass are the basic tools of back-country navigation. Take the time to learn how to use these tools, and your outdoor adventures will become more satisfying.

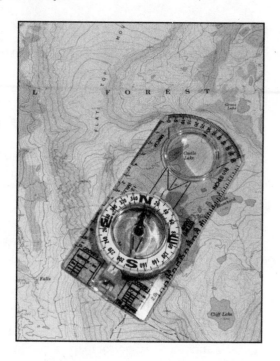

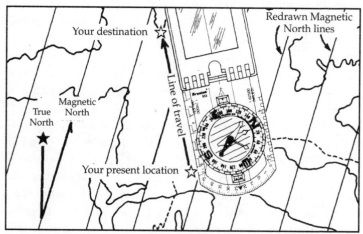

Begin by orienting your map to magnetic north; use your compass and a map on which you've drawn magnetic north lines.

DETERMINING YOUR POSITION BY RESECTION

If two landmarks can be clearly seen and located on the map, your exact position can be determined by resection. Using the compass alone, determine the bearing to each landmark. Then calculate the back bearings by subtracting 180 degrees if the bearing is more than 180 degrees, or adding 180 degrees if the bearing is less than 180 degrees. For example, you can see several mountain peaks in the distance. On your map, you identify the two highest peaks, A and B. The bearing to peak A is 280 degrees, so the back bearing from that peak to your position is 100 degrees (280 minus 180). The bearing to peak B is 340 degrees, so the back bearing is 160 degrees (340 minus 180). To use resection successfully, you have to read the compass very carefully. Double- or triple-check your calculations just to be on the safe side.

The next step is to draw on your map back-bearing lines from the landmarks. Place the compass on one of the landmarks, and orient it so that the needle points to north and the direction-of-travel arrow points to the back bearing to your position. Draw a line following the back bearing. A clear plastic ruler is handy for drawing resection lines. In an emergency, fold one edge of the map over and use it as a straightedge. Repeat the procedure for the other landmark. The point where the two lines intersect is your approximate position. For the above example, you would place the compass on peak A, with the direction-of-travel arrow set at 100 degrees, and rotate the entire compass until the needle lines up with north. Now draw a straight line from the peak at 100 degrees; the direction-of-travel arrow will indicate this direction. Repeat this procedure for peak B, drawing a straight line on a bearing of 160 degrees.

Resection can be used only when distinguishing landmarks can be clearly seen and located on the topographical map. Choosing prominent or unique landmarks will greatly reduce your chances of error.

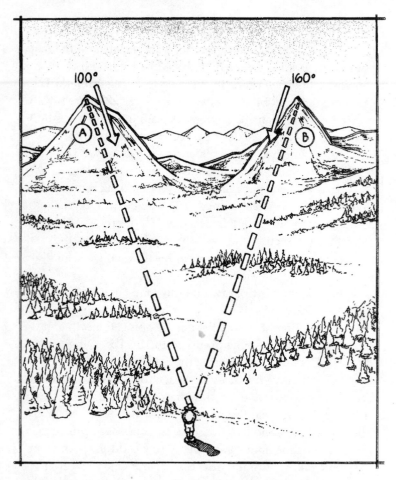

Use resection to determine your position with a map and compass. First locate two prominent landmarks in the distance, and find them on the map. Next, shoot a bearing to these two landmarks. Then calculate a back bearing for each by adding or subtracting 180 degrees. Your position on the map is where the two back-bearing lines intersect.

If you're on a given line such as a river or road, it's a simple matter to cal-culate your position by determining a back bearing from a prominent land feature to your position on that given line. This method is called line posi-tion.

DETERMINING YOUR LOCATION BY LINE POSITION

The second method of determining your present position requires one landmark and that you be on a line of travel you can identify and find on the map, such as a marked trail or a river that you are following. This method is called *line position* because your position is located along a given line. This procedure is similar to resection except that one line is known and you need determine only the other line, from a prominent landmark.

For example, you are following a river but are not certain of your exact position on that river. A tall peak is visible in the distance, and the bearing to its summit is 130 degrees. The back bearing would be 310 degrees. Now orient the map to magnetic north, locate the position of the mountain, and draw a line from that peak at 310 degrees. Your approximate position is where the line intersects the river.

CHECKING YOUR POSITION WITH AN ALTIMETER

You can also check your position by comparing altimeter readings with elevation marks or lines on a topographical map. To do this, however, you must understand how an altimeter operates, have a general idea of your present posi-

A pocket altimeter.

tion, and be able to locate this position on your map. In effect, you're checking your altimeter with the aid of your topographical map.

An altimeter indicates a given altitude by measuring air pressure. At sea level, air pressure is much higher than at 10,000 feet. The barometric cell inside an altimeter expands in low air pressure and contracts in high air pressure. The expansion or contraction of the barometric cell operates the dial of the instrument.

Altimeters have a tendency to give inaccurate readings when the weather is about to change. For example, if you're certain that you're on a mountaintop at 8,000 feet, but your altimeter reads 7,000 feet, it could be because the barometric pressure is rising. Even if you reset your altimeter, the advancing change in weather will affect future readings. Even expensive altimeters tend to give inaccurate readings when the weather is changing. As a result, you have to adjust your altimeter whenever you reach a known elevation. I don't feel that an altimeter is a worthwhile investment (good ones can easily cost several hundred dollars) for the average outdoorsman. You cannot simply look at your altimeter for an elevation reading, find a corresponding elevation on your topographical map, and assume that that's where you are.

USING SECONDARY OBJECTIVES TO DETERMINE POSITION

Accurately determining your position becomes much more difficult when no landmarks can be distinguished. On relatively flat terrain with no high points visible in the distance, in dense forest, or on a cloudy day, resection or line position simply will not be of any value to you. The best you can do is to check your progress against several secondary objectives, and keep track of your direction of travel after you reach each identifiable place. Features such as small streams, cliffs, lakes, and man-made structures serve as good checkpoints. For example, a lake may have a stream entering it at 50 degrees. Provided that there are no other lakes in the vicinity with a

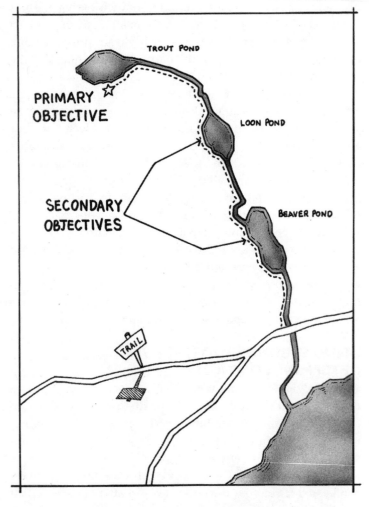

When traveling cross-country, use easily identifiable landmarks—in this case, small ponds connected by a stream—as checks on your progress.

stream running in at 50 degrees, this fact can establish your position.

An entire trip can easily be navigated in this way. A fisherman may be looking for a certain lake in a forest area where the terrain is flat, such as the Adirondack Forest Preserve in upper New York State. He hikes in for one day on a marked trail system and camps at the junction of two marked trails and a stream. He can locate this junction on the map because the Conservation Department has erected a footbridge here. The next morning, he heads off on a compass bearing of 210 degrees for about a half mile and easily finds a small pond. He follows the stream, reaching another small pond and finally a large pond, which was his objective. Using secondary objectives is one trick you can use to check your progress.

STAYING ON COURSE

Once you know your present position and the location of your objective, it's a simple matter to calculate your bearing to that objective. Begin by orienting your map to magnetic north. Locate your position, lay your compass on the map over your position, and note the compass bearing to your objective.

The best type of compass for cross-country travel is the orienteering compass. Simply line up the direction-of-travel arrow with your bearing. When the compass is oriented to magnetic north, the direction-of-travel arrow will point out your heading. If you are inexperienced at cross-country travel, keep your compass handy and check it often. Although checks can be less frequent after you develop some course-following skills, it's a small task to verify your line of travel with a quick check of the compass.

There would be little joy in traveling with one eye on the compass and another on the route. The trick is to pick out landmarks in the distance and on the same heading as your destination. Then you merely have to walk toward it, while

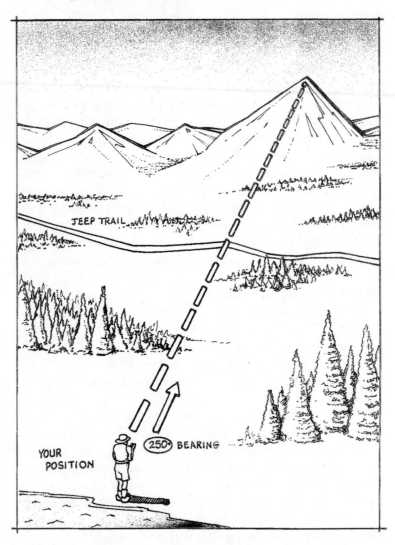

If a prominent land feature such as a mountain lies on a bearing that's the same as (or close to) the bearing you wish to travel, you can use it as a guide. This will make travel easier, as you can stay on course simply by walking toward the land feature rather than having to check your compass often.

taking the terrain into consideration. Let's say you want to take a shortcut to a jeep trail shown on the map to be about 2 miles away on a compass bearing of 250 degrees. First, set the direction-of-travel arrow at 250 degrees. When the compass is oriented to north, you see that a mountain peak also lies at 250 degrees. As long as you can see that peak, you need not check your compass. Simply walk as straight as the terrain will allow toward the mountain peak, and you should cross the jeep trail in less than an hour.

When walking cross-country with a companion, it's much easier to stay on a compass bearing. One partner can serve as the landmark. One hiker stands in one spot, and the other walks in the direction of the bearing, compass in hand. The stationary person should help guide the walker and check his progress with his compass. When the walker reaches the limit of the other's visibility, he stops, and his partner walks to him. Then they can change roles. This technique is ideal for very thick terrain, swamps, marshes, deserts, and anytime visibility is limited or there are no landmarks in the distance.

In open country, both partners can walk at the same time, about 100 yards apart. The front person walks with compass in hand on a predetermined bearing. The rear person follows, periodically checking the accuracy of the lead walker's heading. Because both hikers are aware of the intended bearing, there is little chance of error.

If there's no magic mountain on your compass bearing, you must resort to navigating toward intermediate objectives such as boulders, large trees, or anything else in your line of travel. When you reach that point, take out the compass again, orient it, and sight down the direction-of-travel arrow to find another prominent land feature. Because these checkpoints are nearby, there's the possibility of slight error, but trying to navigate without them can result in having a search party out looking for you.

When you are traveling in relatively flat, featureless terrain, use a hiking companion as a compass-bearing aid.

Natural obstacles can often make straight-line travel to a given destination impossible. If your bearing leads you to the edge of a pond, for example, simply sight across it to a prominent land feature that's in your line of travel, such as a clump of boulders or a large tree; walk around the pond until you reach that point; then head out again on your original course.

Actually, small obstacles are very good checks on your progress. When you plan your route, you should keep an eye out for such obstacles and use them to your advantage. Obviously, large obstacles such as a lake, steep canyon, or cliff should be avoided, but stream junctions, small ponds, or other obstacles that are easy to walk around are good choices. Your route should not be an exercise in detours, but rather as direct a course as possible with built-in, fail-safe checkpoints.

Besides checking the topo, another way to determine the best course of travel is to survey the terrain from a vantage point such as a mountain peak, high ridge line, or other overlook. Even the best eyesight cannot see details in terrain at distances greater than a few hundred yards, so binoculars are a piece of extra equipment worth carrying. Binoculars have many uses on an outdoor trip, and you should consider carrying a pair on every hike. Because they're an important navigational tool, let's take a brief look at the basics.

All binoculars have two numbers separated by an x stamped on the lens housing, such as 8x5. The first number is the magnification of the binoculars. If this number is 8, for example, this means that the magnification of these binoculars is eight power, and an object 120 feet away will appear to be only 15 feet away (120 divided by 8).

The second number indicates the diameter in millimeters of the objective lens. Generally, a larger objective lens diameter lets in more light, gives a brighter image, and allows you to see more clearly in low-light conditions, such as at dusk or dawn, or in a dark forest. If the second number is low, as in

Binoculars are handy for wilderness travel and can help you see the best route to travel over difficult terrain.

8x15, the glasses will be adequate for normal daylight viewing but will be difficult to see through in low light. If the second number is high, as in 8x60, the glasses can almost be considered night binoculars. A good rule of thumb is that a pair of binoculars will be adequate for daylight use if the objective lens diameter is $2^1/_2$ times its magnification—8x20, for example.

There's a wide selection of binoculars to choose from, and you should take your ultimate needs into consideration when shopping. A hunter needs both magnification and light-gathering ability, so 10x35 would be a good choice. A hiker, on the other hand, might find 8x20 more than adequate. Most outdoorsmen also require that the binoculars be compact and lightweight, and there are many good choices on the market. As a rule, stick with the major manufacturers and you can't go wrong. Binoculars made by Nikon, Leitz, Bushnell, Redfield, Swift, Brunton, and Steiner are all of good quality.

ESTIMATING DISTANCE AND TRAVEL TIME

Before starting toward any objective, estimate how long it will take you to get there. If you don't reach your objective in a reasonable amount of time, look for a landmark or land feature against which your progress can be measured. The amount of time that is "reasonable" depends, of course, on terrain, weather, detours, rest stops, stops to cast a fly or photograph scenery, and many other factors. Experienced wilderness travelers develop an ability to estimate this with a fair degree of accuracy.

As a rule, the average hiker carrying a moderate load and in reasonably sound condition can cover about three miles an hour on a marked and cleared trail. Traveling cross-country through forest and brush will reduce this pace by about half. Here your pace will be slower because you will have to pick your way through, around, under, and over obstacles such as fallen trees, boulders, swamps, and underbrush. Dense cover and difficult terrain require not only more time, but they also make estimating difficult. Sometimes the ground will be relatively clear and your pace good, and other times heavy growth will slow your progress. In true wilderness, you also tend to be slowed more by your observations of animals, birds, plants, and the landscape.

Some outdoorsmen use a pedometer to measure distance covered. Worn on the belt, a pedometer records the number of steps taken and indicates distance based on how many of the user's steps equal a quarter mile. All pedometers must be preadjusted to the length of the user's stride. Most record distances up to 25 miles.

In theory, a pedometer is a handy gadget, but on a wilderness trek, it may not be accurate, as your steps will vary in

Pedometer.

length over any ground that is not flat. Steep grades shorten your step; downhill slopes lengthen it. Over broken terrain, such as deadfalls or talus slopes, the length of any one step will be different from all others. A pedometer that could automatically adjust for variations in stride length would be very worthwhile, but to my knowledge no such instrument exists. Instead, I measure and estimate distance on a topographical map.

When traveling cross-country with the aid of a map and compass, the important things to keep track of are your general direction of travel and approximately how long you've been traveling. Estimating distance covered becomes easier as you develop a feel for how long it takes you to cover a given type of terrain. The more you use a topographical map and compass, the more proficient you'll become at determining the best route to follow and estimating the time necessary to cover the distance. As you develop navigational skills, you'll be able to discover true wilderness while always knowing how to find your way back to civilization.

• FIVE •

Planning: The Key to a Successful Outing

One of the best parts of a wilderness trip can take place even before you set foot in the wilderness: the planning. Gathering information, poring over maps, collecting gear, and getting in shape are all important and enjoyable parts of any trip. As a rule of thumb, the time you spend planning should be four times the length of the actual trip, and the more untamed the area, the more crucial this planning stage becomes.

To avoid problems and to get the most out of your wilderness experience, you must plan thoroughly. The more you know about the area you plan to visit, the more likely the trip will live up to your expectations. Planning can easily be accomplished in a few simple steps.

DREAMING UP YOUR IDEAL TRIP

The first step is deciding why you want to make the trip. You may want to fish, hunt, sleep under the stars, or simply get away for a few days. Whatever your motivation, keeping your deepest desire in mind as you plan will increase your chances of coming back satisfied with your experience.

The length of time you have to spend on your trip is a

determining factor in this first stage of planning. If you have just a few days, don't plan on traveling very far from home. If, on the other hand, you have a block of time that exceeds five days, you'll be able to travel farther or simply spend more time in an area that's close by. Your basic reasons for making the trip and the amount of time you have available will combine to help you determine where to go.

Ask yourself whether it will be necessary to leave marked trails to satisfy your needs, or whether you can meet them while staying on one of the many trail systems in the United States. Ninety out of every one hundred hikers in wilderness areas stay on marked trails. The Appalachian Trail in the East and the Pacific Crest Trail in the West are probably the best known and most heavily traveled.

One reason that so many hikers use trail systems is for guidance. It's not difficult to follow a clearly marked trail and not necessary to know anything about magnetic declination, township lines or quadrants, contour intervals, or compass bearings. Rather than navigating with a map and compass, a hiker need only keep an eye out for the next trail marker or ax blaze. The chances of becoming lost are slim, and the outdoor experience can be very worthwhile.

Marked trails cut down on the time you need to spend planning. Little information is necessary other than knowing where the trail ultimately leads. Trail maps are commonly available from the ranger station or headquarters of the area (see the Resources for major listings). These maps show the trail system, lakes, major drainages, roads, landmarks, and points of interest and will often be the only maps you'll need. Many hikers, fishermen, and hunters carry nothing else to guide them and get around the great outdoors quite nicely.

Most hikers like the increased safety of the more heavily traveled marked trails. In case of an emergency, someone can almost always be found, especially during the warm months when many hikers are on the trail.

National forest maps show marked trails and are more than adequate for trail hikes.

Marked trails are often the best way through, around, or over difficult terrain and are easier to hike than untouched wilderness. A bridge or pathway is often built across swamps, streams, and rivers. Mountains can be tackled with a gradual ascent and descent. The trails are maintained so that walking, even when carrying a heavy load, is not as difficult as on a cross-country trek. And while using marked trails, you still can see wildflowers and immense trees, possibly catch more trout than you can eat, and find excellent camping spots and water.

Unfortunately, you'll also see litter and well-beaten pathways. After a day on the trail, you may begin to wonder if anyone wears anything other than Vibram-soled boots. On heavily used trails, you'll have more company—both human and horse—than you may care for.

One sure way to avoid heavily used trails, litter, and other signs of man is to strike out on your own. With 90 percent of the users walking on trails that cover less than 1 percent of any wilderness area, this means that 99 percent of the wilderness is virtually untraveled. Here again, the reason behind your trip should play a big role in your planning. When stepping off the beaten path, you may want to fish some out-of-the-way lakes, hunt in solitude where the really big bucks and bulls are, rise above the crowds, or just leave civilization totally behind for a while. There are risks, of course, but as with most things in life, the greater the risks, the greater the potential for meaningful experiences—in this case a taste of true wilderness.

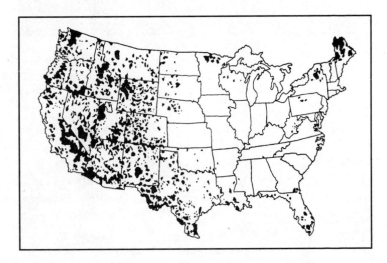

The black areas on the above map represent those areas that can be considered wilderness areas in the "lower forty-eight."

A trip into true wilderness need not totally do without the benefits of marked trail systems. In fact, you can usually use a system to your advantage. Beginning a hike on a trail not only saves you time in entering a wilderness system, but also provides a good jumping-off point. You may, for example, walk in for a day on a marked trail, cut away from the trail at a landmark, then reconnect later with the trail for your trip out.

During your early planning, you also must decide whether to make the trip solo or with one or more companions. Will it be possible to achieve your trip expectations if another person is along on the trip? For cross-country travel, two heads are almost always better than one, especially when both can read a map and compass. Choosing the right companion is not as easy as you might think, however, and should be done with the utmost care. Of no small importance

A companion can enhance an outdoor trip, especially when he or she has some navigational and other wilderness skills.

A wilderness camp is a special place.

is the motivation and experience of the other person. If your companion's experience is not extensive, you may find yourself the navigator, cook, fish cleaner, skinner, camp setter-upper, dish washer, and wood and water hauler. If this is the case, you may not be able to enjoy the trip, unless, that is, you enjoy doing these things for others. Experience has proven to me that a wilderness trip can be enhanced by companions who have developed certain skills, but inexperienced companions tend to make more work and headaches than contributions. So choose any companions with care, as they can make or break your wilderness experience.

OBTAINING AND PREPARING MAPS

The next stage in the planning process is to get the appropriate maps. Begin by checking the state topographical index and deciding which $7\frac{1}{2}$-minute-series topos you'll need. (For information on obtaining these maps, see Topographical Maps in chapter 2.) In many cases you'll be hiking in a familiar area, and you may already have maps of that area. Keep in mind, however, that topographical maps are field-checked and revised periodically. Make sure you have the most current maps available for the area in which you'll be traveling. You can write to the USGS (see Resources) for a listing of sections of the country that are being revised or have been revised since your last visit.

Begin this stage of your planning early enough that you'll have time to look over the maps and become familiar with the area. You may have to mail order your topo maps from the USGS, and this can take several weeks.

If you're planning to hike in a national or state forest, you should also write to the appropriate governing body (see the Resources). Request maps and information on both summer and winter travel in the area, as some agencies designate certain marked trails for travel at specific times of the year—backpacking and snowmobiling, for example. State park maps will not only give you a good general picture, but may also list special regulations for fishing, hunting, boating, and off-road vehicles. In many cases, these maps will contain information that is found nowhere else, such as which areas receive a lot of traffic and which remain virtually untouched.

Advance planning for a wilderness trip in some cases may be an absolute necessity. With so many people on national forest trails year-round, the USFS is restricting some access by requiring wilderness travel permits for some areas, especially during the summer months. It may take an entire year to get reservations for a trip to the Grand Tetons, for example. In that case, only half the permits can be reserved and purchased in advance, and the rest are first come, first served.

Write to the ranger office of the area you're planning to visit and ask whether permits are required and, if they are, how to go about getting one.

Fishing and hunting licenses can usually be purchased by mail from state fish and game departments. Some western rivers have restrictions, and fish and game departments can also inform you of any special regulations and required permits, stamps, or licenses.

Once you've obtained maps of the area you plan to visit, study them to choose the right wilderness area that will satisfy your objections. For hunting, keep in mind that the bigger deer and elk are most common in the high country; for fishing, look for an isolated pond or stream; for grand views, stick

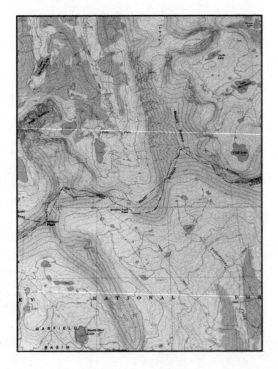

A lot can be learned about an area before you get there by studying a topographical map.

to the higher elevations; for exploring, head toward an interesting-looking site, such as an old miner's cabin. An ironclad itinerary isn't necessary, but you should have some specific goals in mind. This is especially important if you plan to leave marked trails, because navigating with map and compass requires an objective. At this point in your pretrip planning, you may also want to look for good campsites and routes to take advantage of terrain.

Magazine articles describing wilderness outings are also good sources of information in planning your trip. They often include maps of the area visited and useful bits of information.

Part of the planning stage involves preparing your maps for the trip. Draw magnetic declination lines on your topos while you still have the kitchen table as a large, flat work surface. You need to provide some protection for your maps. Even though map paper stock is heavy, it can be damaged by the elements. One very good method used to toughen up topographical maps—even if you plan to carry them in a protective case—is to apply a plastic coating. A clear plastic spray, such as Krylon, is ideal. Spray both sides of the map for optimum protection and sealing. Topographical maps protected in this manner will stand up to abuse for several seasons. In time, you may need to recoat sections of the map, especially if you fold rather than roll the map. Be sure to draw the magnetic declination lines on the map before coating.

Another method is to laminate your map between two sheets of clear plastic. This method requires that the map be cut into several useful sections; 8-by-10-inch pieces work well. Glue the pieces back-to-back, then sandwich them between larger sheets of adhesive-backed clear plastic. Large copy centers can do this for you at a small charge. This coating is ideal, as you can write on the surface with a grease pencil or crayon to indicate routes, campsites, and so forth, and wipe it clean after the trip.

*Coat your topo-
graphical maps
with plastic spray;
this will protect
them in the field.*

Before you begin cutting up your topographical maps, think carefully about how to best divide the map. Also choose carefully which pieces to glue back-to-back, so that the sections can be laid out for a coherent overview of the area if needed. There are several cases in which this method of map protection may not be suitable—if you are hiking over a large area, for example, or if cutting the map will obscure or eliminate important land features. On the other hand, this technique works well if you're planning to limit your travels to a relatively small area or if you're cutting up a 15-minute-series topographical map.

Probably the most popular way to protect maps in the field is to carry them in a map case. Basically there are two types for field use: a cylindrical tube with waterproof caps, which holds up to four maps; and a flat map case (which holds one map) with one or both sides constructed of clear plastic.

A flat map case is probably the more useful for protecting a single map. Several types are available in hiking-equipment and surveyor shops. Any good flat map case will comfortably hold a folded topographical map and enable the user to view a respectable section. The flat map case is generally sealed by way of a plastic Zip-lock arrangement along the top edge.

It's possible to make your own flat map case from clear plastic and tape, but homemade map cases leave a lot to be desired. They usually leak, and they do not lend themselves to getting at the map without taking the case apart. In the

Flat and tube map cases can carry other things in addition to maps.

long run, it's better to spend the small amount of money to buy a map case.

There are many times when you should take both types of map cases along—the flat map case to hold the map you're using, and the tube case to carry and protect your other maps. You can often find other uses for both types of cases as well. For example, my telescoping fishing rod fits inside my tube case, and my fishing license and notepad fit inside the flat map case.

GETTING IN SHAPE

Your physical condition will have a direct bearing on how much you will enjoy your outing. Hiking with a loaded backpack is more exercise than most of us usually get, so even if you are in reasonably good physical condition, you should do a few things during the planning stage to ensure that you'll be able to go the distance without too much suffering. Many experts recommend beginning an exercise program several weeks before your trip. This might include jogging for a short period several times a week, doing some type of exercise at home on a daily basis, visiting a local spa or fitness center to add a little muscle tone to your body. If you're in good shape before you start on your trip, you'll enjoy the experience much more than if you're not.

Don't overlook your feet when getting the rest of your body into shape. Most people seem to believe that they can just lace up a pair of hiking boots and take off. Unfortunately, this can lead to overexertion and blisters. Most of us are not accustomed to wearing heavy hiking boots and usually purchase a pair of lightweight walkers. Keep in mind, however, that even lightweight boots need to be broken in properly. You should wear your hiking boots around town for at least several weeks before your trip. Wiping your bare feet with a cloth dampened in rubbing alcohol can also help toughen your feet. Do this twice a day for about two weeks prior to your trip.

CHOOSING GEAR

Another part of the planning stage is assembling gear. When choosing gear for a wilderness trip, there are many considerations, including the time of year, the length of the trip, and any special objectives, such as hunting, fishing, or photography. If you plan to leave the trails and strike off on your own, keep in mind that an internal-frame backpack is much better suited for off-trail use than a conventional external-frame pack. Hiking boots should lace up above the ankle for added support on tough terrain.

You'll also need some means of carrying water—ideally one container that can carry greater amounts for camp use, and a lighter, smaller one for use on the trail.

To ensure that you'll have enough water, plan your route to take advantage of springs, streams, ponds, and lakes. On a typical summer hike, you should drink at least 1 gallon of water per day. You should know where you can find water at any given time, as well as carrying a supply in your pack.

In even the most remote wilderness areas, you run the risk of contracting a stomach parasite caused by giardiasis from drinking untreated water, so you should not drink any water unless it has been treated or run through some type of filtration system. Be sure to carry water purification tablets, water filtration equipment, or both so that you can be sure the water you drink will not cause any serious internal problems.

Another area that will require a bit of thoughtful planning is the food you will carry along. Generally speaking, the longer the trip, the fewer the choices in the food department. If your hike is not too long, say less than three days, and there are several members in the party, you can pack just about any kind of food. If your plans call for wandering for four or more

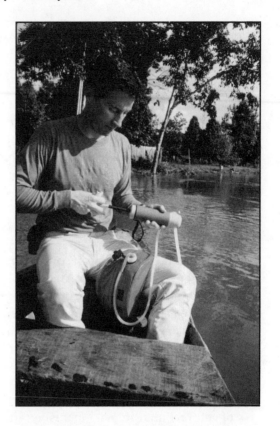

Water purification or filtering gear should always be used in the wilderness. (Courtesy PUR Drinking Water Systems.)

days, however, you must take foods that are lightweight and compact.

There is a huge selection of freeze-dried foods currently available in backpacking-equipment and sporting-goods stores. Add to this the even greater (and generally lower-priced) offerings at your local supermarket, and you should have little problem planning meals that are tasty, lightweight, and easy to prepare.

As a guideline for meal planning, you should strive for an intake of 2,000 to 3,000 calories per day. You will burn this many calories in a single day of hiking during the summer. In winter, you will easily burn twice as many calories. All food manufacturers are now required to list nutritional information (calories, fat, carbohydrates, protein) on the packaging; you can use this information to aid you in your meal planning. Many outdoor books have chapters on meal planning and nutrition, and there are whole cookbooks devoted to foods for backpacking, as well.

Also give careful thought to the clothing you'll need. Some wilderness areas, such as parts of the Northwest and the Northeast, get more than a fair share of rainfall during the summer months; other areas, such as the Southwest, receive almost none, except during late August through September. If there's a possibility of foul weather, carry rain gear—a poncho or jacket and pants. Rain suits made with Gore-Tex are expensive but extremely lightweight and far superior to the old heavy rubber and canvas rain suits. Gore-Tex is a breathable, waterproof laminate, and any rain garment laminated with Gore-Tex will not only keep you dry, but will also allow your skin to breathe.

Warm clothing is another requirement, even when hiking in the summer. This is especially true if your hike takes you above 9,000 feet in elevation, where temperatures can easily drop into the low thirties during the night. At higher elevations, snow is possible any month of the year. Always be prepared for cool or cold weather if there is even a remote possibility. The best choices include a pullover wool sweater or down jacket (lightweight and stuffable), a synthetic jacket, or fiberpile garments.

It's important to dress for the terrain you'll be walking over. Rugged clothing is in order for heavy brush or rocky country where you may be spending part of your time on your knees or the seat of your pants. Probably the best (and

Rain gear is essential in some areas.

paradoxically the worst) choice of clothing for the bottom half of your body is a pair of blue jeans. A frequent choice, jeans are tough but also are rough on the skin and slightly restrictive, especially when the terrain requires stepping high. They also tend to dry slowly. In the colder months you should not wear blue jeans, because they will not dry if they become wet, and this will cause you to lose precious body heat. A surprising number of hypothermia cases result from wearing blue jeans, occasionally even during the summer months, as even a light breeze can reduce the air temperature.

When the weather is warm, many people wear shorts, which makes alot of sense when traveling on well-beaten paths. When you are striking off cross-country, however, it's best to protect your legs. Brush, rocks, and insects can all contribute to tearing up the skin on your bare legs, so it makes more sense to wear long pants when you're blazing your own trail.

During the spring and summer, no matter where in the

	Wind Chill Equivalent Temperatures, Degrees Farenheit									
Estimated Wind Speed				**Actual Thermometer Reading**						
	50	40	30	20	10	0	-10	-20	-30	-40
Calm	50	40	30	20	10	0	-10	-20	-30	-40
5	48	37	27	16	6	-5	-15	-26	-36	-47
10	40	28	16	4	-9	-21	-33	-46	-58	-70
15	36	22	9	-5	-18	-36	-45	-58	-72	-85
20	32	18	4	-10	-25	-39	-53	-67	-82	-96
25	30	16	0	-15	-29	-44	-59	-74	-88	-104
30	28	13	-2	-18	-33	-48	-63	-79	-94	-109
35	27	11	-4	-20	-35	-49	-67	-82	-98	-113
40	26	10	-6	-21	-37	-53	-69	-85	-100	-116

To use this chart, find the approximate wind speed in the left column, and the actual temperature along the top row. The equivalent temperature is located where these two intersect. For example, at a wind speed of 10 mph and a temperature of 30 degrees, the windchill is 16 degrees.

United States you travel, months you'll encounter biting insects. Some parts of the country have only a handful, but other areas have squadrons. Spring in many areas is blackfly season, and it's also a time for tick activity. Later in the season, through summer, you'll encounter mosquitoes. Heavily wooded forests with ample watersheds are ideal breeding grounds for biting insects. Insect repellent can help protect you from these pests. There are several types on the market that work with varying degrees of success. Choose one with a high percentage of the chemical deet or, if you prefer a natural (nonchemical) insect repellent, try Natrapel (from Tender Corp.).

Other gear you might plan to take along includes a tent, bedding, a foam pad, a first-aid kit, a rope, a small stove and fuel, a flashlight, a camera and film, fishing equipment, a firearm and ammunition, and whatever else you might need to help you enjoy your wilderness experience. Volumes have been written about what gear to bring along, and you should consult these if you are at all unsure. Equipment shops can also be of great help for the novice.

Find out in advance if any will be special restrictions will be in effect for the area you plan to visit; this could affect what you carry. For example, in western Montana during the summer of 1994, open fires were not permitted in the backcountry because of the danger of wildfires. As a result, hikers were required to carry stoves for cooking.

Pretrip planning, from choosing the area to assembling gear, is an important part of any wilderness experience. If you plan thoroughly, you'll increase your chances of having an enjoyable trip. Poor planning, on the other hand, can lead to disaster.

When you do begin your trip be sure to leave word of your destination, probable route, and expected time of return.

Many trail systems in national forests have a register at the trailhead in which you list the number in your party, planned length of stay, and destination. Take the time to enter this information; it may help searchers find you in an emergency. Most of all, enjoy your trip. Your pretrip planning and map and compass skills should enable you to do just that.

· SIX ·

In the Field

Newspapers regularly carry stories of hikers, hunters, fishermen, and snowmobilers who were lost or injured while in the outdoors. In many cases the poor fellow or gal spent a few uncomfortable nights without food, got eaten alive by biting insects, and was finally found by a search party. Others were not so lucky.

Many of these unfortunate experiences probably could have been avoided if the hiker had a basic understanding of map and compass use and could deal with navigational and weather problems, either by realizing that a problem existed (and thus being prepared to deal with it) or by choosing another route. Often good old common sense can solve a problem before it really becomes one.

NEGOTIATING NATURAL OBSTACLES

More often than not, the problems you'll encounter while traveling cross-country are related to getting around, over, or through obstacles in your path. Most common are having to cross rivers, streams, and lakes, and climb steep inclines such as a rock face or cliff. Let's look at some of the better ways to get past these natural obstacles.

The only practical ways to cross a river or stream are to walk over a bridge, wade, or swim. In most cases a bridge will not be handy—unless you find a large, sturdy tree that has conveniently fallen across—so you'll most likely have to choose between wading and swimming.

When wading across a river or stream, there are several things you should do to avoid mishap. First, scout along the riverbank to find the best place to cross. Good choices are areas that are wide and not very deep—less than 3 feet—and places where many rocks are exposed above the surface. Ideally, these spots will also be on a straight rather than curved part of the river. Poor choices include still, deep pools; large rapids; and narrow places with fast moving water.

Once you've located a suitable crossing site, find a strong stick or pole to serve as a staff. This will make you more stable, as three legs are better than two when crossing a river. Use it to feel the bottom and to help you find the best places to step.

Before you step into the river, unfasten your pack's hip belt and loosen your pack straps. If you should fall into the water while attempting to cross, your pack will act like an anchor and drag you down as you are pulled by the current. If you do go down, you must shuck your pack so that you can regain your footing or swim to shore. If possible, swim with one hand on the pack. If not, get yourself to safety and worry about the pack later.

You'll find wading much easier if you leave your boots on. They will get soaked, to be sure, but they'll give you better footing on slippery rocks. You may, however, want to remove your socks, until you've safely crossed.

If the current is strong, cross at a downstream angle rather than straight across. Always move slowly, making sure of your footing before transferring weight from one foot to another. If you start moving too fast, you may get caught up in the current, lose your footing, and fall.

If there are several members in the hiking party and you have a long rope, another approach is to let one member cross without a pack and tie one end of the rope to a tree or other suitable anchor on the far side. Then each member of the party can cross with one hand on the rope for balance, stability, and safety. If you use this method, remember that it is safer to be on the downriver side of the rope than upriver. Again, loosen pack straps and unfasten the hip belt so that you can remove the pack if necessary.

If the river or body of water that you want to cross is more than 3 feet deep and wading is not possible, you'll either have to swim across or not cross at this point. It's impossible to swim with a pack on your back, so if you decide to swim, you must have some means of floating your gear across. The best choice is an air mattress. Another possibility, if you're a fisherman, is a float tube.

Before plunging in, determine whether swimming will be safe. If the water temperature is less than 50 degrees, as with many mountain rivers, you would be in danger of hypothermia, a lowering of the body temperature. If a river is very swift, you may not be able to swim across. Let common sense and good judgment be your guide in all cases.

Also consider that the water level of a mountain river is usually lower early in the day. By afternoon rivers are often swollen with melted snow. As a result, a crossing that is far too dangerous in the afternoon may be possible in the morning.

Another common obstacle on a wilderness trip is steep inclines. Your experience will be your best guide when you're faced with such obstacles. If you have even the slightest touch of acrophobia, it's best to avoid any form of climbing. The more cross-country travel you do, the greater the odds that sooner or later you'll come up against a steep incline. It is therefore to your distinct advantage to know basic rock craft and carry some basic climbing gear to help you navigate up and down.

Mountaineering has its own set of equipment, techniques, knots, body stances, signals, and safety considerations. Since this information is much too important to be briefly touched on here, I suggest that you seek guidance—from books and manuals, and through personal instruction—before you make any attempt at technical climbing.

The advantages of knowing some of the basics of rock climbing are obvious. A party with a rope—and the required know-how to use it—has few limitations. Peaks or high mountain lakes that are inaccessible to most hikers because of steep rock are within easy reach of a party with climbing equipment and experience.

Many wilderness travelers carry a length of rope without any intentions of scaling sheer rock faces. This makes a lot of sense, as a rope can prove its worth even on moderate inclines. I routinely carry about 50 feet of 9-millimeter braided nylon climbing rope and use it for hauling up gear and for hanging a food bag up high when in bear country.

When bushwhacking through tough terrain, look for game trails. These trails often provide a pathway through seemingly impenetrable brush and timber. Big-game animals spend most of their waking hours in search of food and water, and they wander almost constantly over a given range or territory. Since they are very much creatures of habit, these woodland animals travel along familiar routes that lead through browse areas. In most cases these well-beaten paths will prove to be the best way through an area, because these animals don't make traveling any harder than need be. You may have to duck and crawl at times, but they can save hours of strenuous trail blazing.

Deer, elk, sheep, and moose trails are not difficult to locate. Most commonly you'll find them traversing hillsides, leading through thick brush or timber, negotiating saddle or mountain passes, or following ridge lines. If you can find a game trail that goes in the direction you plan to travel, by all means use it, but keep your compass handy for checking along the way.

Game trails often have a way of ending abruptly. If you are following such a trail and it seems to peter out, try to relocate it by looking 10 to 15 yards uphill or downhill from the original trail.

TRAVELING BY NIGHT

Hiking in the dark is very different from hiking in the daylight. Travel in the dark is much slower. The inability to see very far, coupled with unfamiliar terrain, eats up time faster than distance. Experienced outdoorsmen agree that traveling at night is risky and should be avoided whenever possible. Unfortunately, in an emergency, you may have no choice. You may have to seek emergency help for a companion, get out of the backcountry before a blizzard or other weather disaster strikes, or continue after sunset to arrive at a prearranged checkpoint or shelter.

There are a few things you should know so that you'll be able to navigate in the dark if necessary. Most important is to stay calm and rational. If you are ever in doubt about the right direction or if you reach an obstacle, stop and wait until it's light enough to see a solution. Walk carefully to avoid injuries caused by poor footing or being hit in the face by branches or brush.

At night, traveling with one eye on the compass becomes necessary, as secondary objectives and other landmarks cannot be seen distinctly. The best type of compass for night travel is an orienteering compass with a luminous dial. With-

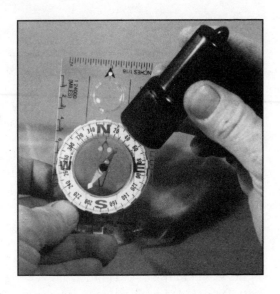

Charge up the dial on your compass with a flashlight, and you'll be able to read it in the dark.

out the luminous dial, you will have to turn a flashlight on and off for every compass reading, which seriously impairs your night vision. Also, the electromagnet in the flashlight may influence the compass reading. To charge a luminous dial, place it on the lens of a lit flashlight for about one minute. The numbers and lines on the dial will stay visible for several hours.

Before setting out into the night, be certain of your compass bearing. Proceed on course very carefully. Night navigation is best accomplished by several people. The leader sets the pace and follows a bearing, while the others follow and at the same time check the accuracy of the direction of travel with their own compasses. As the leader is under the most stress, it makes sense to rotate this responsibility.

Nocturnal animals are the very least of the nighttime dangers, as they will usually hear you coming and take off into the night. The biggest dangers come from the inability to see close land features easily. In flat, open terrain, this may not be much of a problem, but in a forest, black shadows will hide the best places to step. The only safe approach is to walk at a slow pace and choose your steps carefully.

In particularly tough terrain, by all means use a flashlight, but keep in mind that your night vision will suffer. To cut down on the adjustment your eyes have to make each time you turn it on and off, cover half or three-quarters of the lens with a piece of tape.

You'll be amazed at how well you can see in the dark. Unless the sky is overcast, the stars alone provide much natural light. On a night with a full moon, you can see a good distance. Although vision is always somewhat impaired in the dark, hearing, touch, and smell become more acute. Try to take advantage of this shift. You may notice a coolness in the air and the sound of rushing water before you see a stream, for example. Rely on your senses, as they are usually right.

A group should travel single file. A piece of white tape or other bright marking on each person's back will make following easier. Try to stay on a marked trail for night travel, as trail markers are often made from reflective material that is easy to spot in the dark.

WEATHER

Weather can make or break a wilderness trek, and when you're in the field, you need to be able to anticipate changes. In the wilderness, some simple tools and observations will enable you to do so. Signs of change include cloud patterns, wind shifts, and air pressure. At the least, weather signs can tell you that some change is coming, which is often more important than knowing what the change will be. Farmers and sailors develop a sixth sense about the weather, and with careful observation and a little scientific background, you can too.

When planning your trip, take into consideration the area's probable weather patterns. Some parts of the country are generally dry, and others wet. Some areas are usually cooler than others. The altitude, the time of year, the general wind direction, and whether the sun's rays strike the area all combine to produce weather for a given area. High mountains or large bodies of water can create their own weather. Area residents and newspapers are the best sources for local weather information. Also keep in mind that regional weather patterns, while often unique, follow the general weather pattern of North America.

By gathering as much information as possible from local media just before a trip, you can guess at the short-term weather picture. You'll get more out of a weather report if you know some basics and understand the terminology.

Weather maps often show the leading edges of warm or cold air masses, called *fronts*. It's the movement of these air masses that generates weather. You'll be a better weather predictor if you understand how these air masses come into being. As the sun's rays beat down unevenly on the earth's surface, the air above certain areas heats up, expands, and then rises, because warm air is less dense and lighter than cold air. As warm air rises, cold air from surrounding areas that did not receive as much heat from the sun rushes in to fill the void created by the upward-moving warm air. This is a simplified version of how a weather cycle develops, but nevertheless it explains how air masses begin to move.

As air masses enter the continental United States, they move eastward, because the earth rotates from east to west. This midlatitude wind belt is called the *prevailing westerlies*. The colder air from the north drifts southeast, and the warmer tropical air masses move northeast. Often weather maps show a cold northern air mass moving southeast on a collision course with a warm, southern, northeast-moving air mass.

Since warm air is less dense than cold air, it has the ability to pick up and hold moisture as the air mass moves over land and water. When a moving warm air mass (warm front) meets

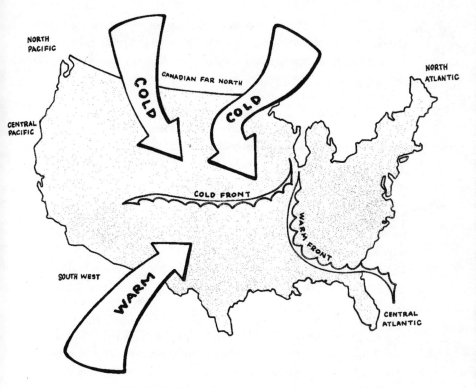

*Weather in the United States is produced by the actions of air masses origi-
nating in six broad areas.*

a moving cold air mass (cold front), some of the moisture in
the warm air condenses and falls as rain.

At any moment, air masses are moving toward or away
from the United States, and they cause all possible types of
weather. Nevertheless, when the weatherman describes a certain movement, the prevailing westerly phenomenon and
characteristics generally associated with the six primary air
masses can suggest the probable result.

Pacific polar maritime air refers to air masses that originate in the North Pacific and travel southeast along the Alaskan coast. They bring year-round good visibility, broken skies, low temperatures, and when moving inland, precipitation.

High arctic air, or *polar continental air,* comes from the Canadian far north. In winter, it brings very dry and cold air, very good visibility, almost cloudless skies, and often high winds. In summer, it brings cool, dry air. Summer arctic air often causes cloudy afternoons along the border between the United States and Canada.

North Atlantic air masses usually stay offshore, but they do blow in occasionally. When they do, New Englanders call them *Northeasters,* and suffer cold, raw, cloudy weather in winter and clammy weather in summer.

The *central Pacific air mass* is also maritime, but it is tropical. In winter, it is characterized by overcast skies, high humidity, warmth, and generally poor visibility. Central Pacific air masses shift direction during the summer months as a result of a change in the earth's position relative to the sun. Some air masses move only during certain seasons of the year, and this is one of them.

Southwest air masses originate in the semiarid plateaus of Mexico and the Southwest. In summer, they bring dry cloudless weather with hot days. In winter, they are warm but usually accompanied by clouds and can be a prediction of a storm to come from the north.

Atlantic tropical maritime air originates in the central Atlantic. Like its Pacific equivalent, it brings warm, moist air in winter and high humidity in summer. It moves north up the east coast and usually causes storms and hurricanes in the autumn.

As a rule, you can foretell changes in weather by noting changes in air pressure. A barometer, which measures barometric pressure (simply air pressure), can be of some value in the wilderness. A high-pressure system is relatively heavy with moisture. It is also probably warm, because warm air can hold more moisture than cool air can. A low-pressure system, on the other hand, carries less moisture and is probably cool.

The very accurate barometers used by meteorologists are the mercurial type. These barometers are laboratory instruments that stand many feet tall and are not portable. They consist of a glass tube filled with mercury and are closed at the bottom. The top curves upward and is exposed to the atmosphere. High air pressure pushes the mercury up the tube; low pressure lets it fall down.

Much more portable, and accurate enough for amateur weather predicting, is an aneroid barometer. Its basic part is a vacuum chamber that is depressed under high air pressure and expands under low atmospheric pressure. A needle indicates the pressure. If a second scale is put on the instrument, it can serve as an altimeter as well, as changes in air pressure due to altitude are measured by an altimeter the same way. Several backpacking-equipment companies offer pocket altimeter-barometers, starting at around $50. I feel, however, that although a barometer may work well on a wall in your home, it is really more trouble than it's worth on a wilderness trek. A barometer is most useful in a stationary position and at a constant altitude. Nevertheless, many hikers carry pocket barometers.

Since a change in altitude will also read like a change in barometric pressure, always be sure that the aneroid barometer is stationary when you take readings from it. Changes in barometric pressure are clues to coming weather changes. A falling barometer (rising altimeter) usually means improved weather. Also, in general, a rapid change in barometric pressure indicates that the change in weather will not last long, but a slow change in barometric pressure means that the weather conditions on the way will last for a while.

A thermometer is a handy instrument for wilderness

weather predicting. The temperature in camp can indicate a number of things: whether there is a chance of snow; whether it will be safe to leave freezable foods and liquids outside shelter; whether game will be on the move (deer and other big game move more in cold weather); whether aquatic insects will be hatching or flying. Any thermometer for wilderness travel should be lightweight and as indestructible as possible. There are many inexpensive models that are adequate. The thermometer I carry measures both air and water temperature.

Another type of thermometer records both high and low

This Brunton compass has a built-in thermometer.

temperatures. With this type of thermometer, you can determine how cold it dropped during the night without having to go outside the tent to check in the middle of the night.

Clouds are important to weather forecasting because they signal changes and indicate movement of air masses. By keeping an eye on cloud movement (or lack of it) during the course of a day, you can make fair weather predictions. For example, if there are high, wispy clouds or no clouds in the sky, the weather will probably remain clear. If later in the day the clouds look like puffy, white masses, the weather will remain fair. But if during the day the clouds seem to be getting lower or darker, or if the sky takes on a gray cast, start looking for shelter, or at least get ready to break out your rain gear.

Clouds are visible evidence that there's some moisture in the air. On cold, dry days there will be few clouds; on warm, humid days there will be many, and often the sky will be completely overcast. The following are some basic guidelines to reading the clouds.

Cirrus clouds are high and thin, often looking like filmy wisps. They frequently form the leading edge of a warm front as it rides over a colder air mass and usually indicate a change in weather within two days.

Cumulus clouds are puffy, billowy, and white with flat, gray bottoms. Cumulus clouds are fair-weather clouds that form on warm afternoons after the sun has heated up the earth's surface and caused moist air to rise. They usually disappear as the earth cools in the evening. Cumulus clouds are commonly large and distinctive when they appear alone but change when combined with other forms.

Stratus clouds are solid, gray masses more than distinctive clouds and are responsible for days of drizzling rain. Stratus clouds are formed in layers.

Although any one of these cloud types can appear alone, more often than not they will be combined or occur at heights

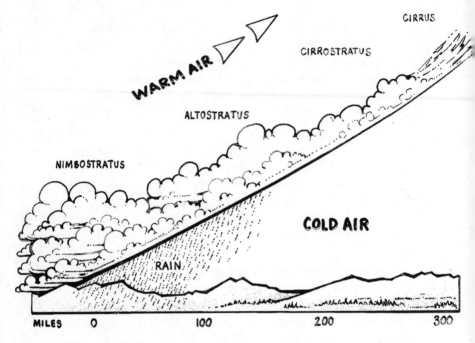

The advance of a warm front usually follows a set pattern. The above illustration shows a warm front moving from left to right.

not associated with their basic types. This makes cloud identification much more complicated, and there's a whole vocabulary built around this.

Alto, for example, is put before cumulus or stratus to indicate that the clouds are higher than their usual level but still below the cirrus level. *Altocumulus* clouds have the characteristics of the cumulus family but are at a height just below cirrus clouds. *Altostratus* clouds are gray layered masses that often obscure the sun or moon.

Nimbus clouds are rain-bearing clouds. *Nimbostratus* clouds are low, thickly layered cloud masses often considered the true rain clouds. *Cumulonimbus* clouds are towering thunderheads with distinctive anvil-shaped tops and dark, moving bottoms. Cumulonimbus clouds are accompanied by thunder and lightning and rain, hail, or snow flurries.

When attempting to predict the weather, it's also worth paying heed to common knowledge or folklore, especially when it's given by someone who has spent a lifetime in an area and passed much time outdoors. Many folk maxims are right on the mark and hold up when viewed through the trained eye of a meteorologist as well.

One such saying is this:

Evening red and morning gray
Help the traveler on his way.
Evening gray and morning red
Bring rain down upon his head.

A meteorologist would probably agree, considering that our North American weather travels west to east—the prevailing westerlies—and that the sun's rays (either rising or setting) pass over the earth in straight lines. If the setting sun's rays pass through dry air, which always contains many small dust particles, the effect is a reddish sunset. If, however, the last rays of the sun encounter moisture-laden air, they will not pass through, and the effect will be a grayish sunset with little or no red. Therefore, a red sunset means that dry air is coming from the west, and a gray sunset means that moisture-laden air is moving toward you.

And as the corollary to that, if the first rays of the sun strike moisture-laden air in the east, but there is no moisture-filled air in the west, the sunrise will appear gray. Because the weather in the east has already passed, it may be safe to assume that the day's weather will be good. On the other hand, if the first rays pass through dry air in the east and there is moisture-laden air in the west, the reddish effect will be reflected by the moisture-filled air in the west—a dramatic sunrise.

Dew in the morning is another weather indicator:

When the dew is on the grass,
Rain will never come to pass.
When the grass is dry at morning light,
Look for rain before the night.

Dew is moisture formed when warm air settles onto the earth after the earth has cooled during the night. Early fall, September particularly, is a good time for dew, as the days are warm and the nights cool. The presence of dew means that the earth has cooled enough that fair weather will follow. If a cloud cover moves in during the night, the earth is blanketed, keeping the warm air close to the surface. Thus the earth will not cool, and dew will not form. If a cold front moves in, there will be no dew because cold air contains little moisture.

Barometric pressure causes a number of things to happen in nature, and if you're observant, you can predict a weather change simply by watching the world around you. For example, in the low barometric pressure before a rainstorm, the leaves of some trees, which are dry, turn upside down—perhaps to better catch the moisture in the air. Mosquitoes and gnats feed more heavily when the barometric pressure is low, and fish will feed heavily near the surface of the water because insect hatches often occur just before a storm, perhaps triggered by low pressure. Smoke from a campfire will fall to the ground, rather than rise straight up, in high barometric pressure because it is less dense than the moisture-laden air above; in effect, the smoke is forced to the ground by air pressure.

Some old-timers claim to be able to smell a storm coming. The smell of deep woods, small ponds, marshes, and swamps is caused by gases formed by rotting vegetation. When the weather is fair, the barometric pressure is high and keeps these gases in close to the earth's surface. Before a storm, the low air pressure allows more gases and odors to rise from the earth, and the air smells different.

Any old salt will tell you that gulls sit in the water or on docks or rocks when a storm is coming. This is probably because it is more difficult for a bird to fly when the barometric pressure is low than during a high-pressure spell. A gull flying inland indicates a brewing storm, whereas a gull flying out to open sea means fair weather.

You can also determine wind direction by observing water birds. Ducks, gulls, loons, and other water birds always sit on the water facing the wind, and they land or take off into the wind.

When all is said and done, the weather will do what it wants to do, and your guess is as good as anyone else's. When making these guesses, though, never rely on a single sign or instrument. A meteorologist uses many instruments and many weather theories. An old-timer will watch for as many natural signs as possible. As a wilderness traveler, you should become as informed as possible about weather and learn the signs that indicate weather change.

WHAT TO DO IF YOU GET LOST

Occasionally, even outdoorsmen who have mastered the basics of map and compass get turned around a bit. If you ever find yourself in such a position, probably the most important thing to remember is to remain calm. Stop walking, sit down, and break out your map and compass. Use resection, line position, or both to determine your position (see chapter 4).

Once you've determined your position, you can decide on your next course of action. Pick an objective, determine a bearing, and then proceed toward it. Choose clear secondary objectives—prominent land features such as springs, valleys, or ponds—along the route so that you can be positive of your progress.

Occasionally, poor visibility will make this impossible. If the condition seems temporary, it is probably best to wait until you can see distant land features clearly, then walk out on a predetermined course. If poor visibility seems like it will last for more than about eight hours, you must decide if you want to wait that long or move on now and use your map and compass to help you navigate.

With a map and compass, the chances are small that you'll ever become truly lost in any wilderness area in the continental United States. The more you know about an area before you go into it, the better able you will be to find your way out. Here again, thorough planning can pay off. Before your trip, commit to memory certain facts about the area, such as the approximate location of large rivers, mountain ranges, or other prominent natural features. Also note their relationship to roads and other marks of civilization, as well as the direction of flow of any rivers or streams.

In the event that you feel you are totally lost—which is just about impossible if you've been using your map and compass correctly—your best bet is to stay put. This may also be necessary if you become injured. If you've left word with responsible folks back in civilization as to where you'll be wandering and the expected time of your return, it's a fair assumption that they will notify the proper authorities and a search will be initiated. You must have faith that in time you'll be discovered by a rescue party.

In the meantime, explore the general vicinity. Without wandering very far from your position, try to find a field, meadow, or large body of water. If you can find such a place, relocate to this spot so that you will be more visible to an air search party.

Your chances of being spotted are much greater if you can create an unnatural-looking symbol on the ground that can be easily seen from the air. This is also an excellent approach if a member of a hiking party is injured and requires medical atten-

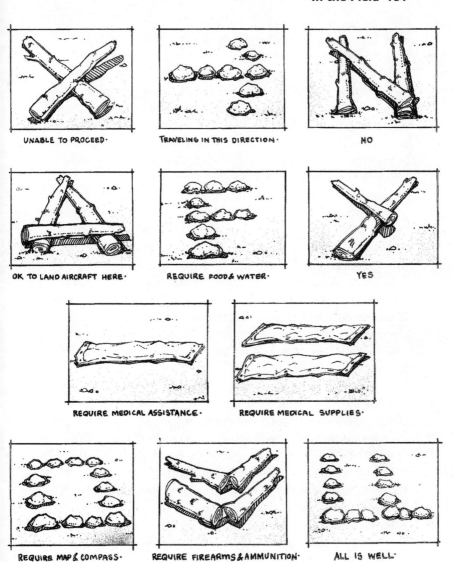

International ground-to-air signals.

tion. One or more members of the party should stay with the injured hiker while one or more of the others go for help. Help most often arrives in a helicopter, so by marking the location, you help the rescue aircraft spot the area much more easily. Know in advance that many federal and state search-and-rescue teams now charge for their time spent locating lost or injured hikers. Even if you never find yourself in a situation where you require some type of assistance from above, someday you may discover another hiker in need of some help. This is reason enough to know some ground-to-air symbols.

A long panel means that you need medical assistance. Two long parallel panels indicate that you require medical supplies. A large X means that you are unable to proceed. An arrow pointing in one direction indicates the route you have headed on. A large triangle means that it is probably safe to land an aircraft in the area. If you need food or water, a large F is the symbol. A large square means that you need a map and compass (shame on you!). VV means that you need firearms and ammunition. N means no, Y means yes, and LL means all is well.

Another way to signal for help is a flare-type distress signal. Several backpacking-equipment companies now sell various signals that are similar to pistols or flares used by seamen except that they are much smaller, less expensive, lighter in weight, and safer. Distress signals are usually self-contained flares with some type of firing mechanism that shoots the flare (commonly brilliant red or international orange) 100 to 150 feet up into the sky. If you're in trouble and an air search is looking for you, some type of emergency flare might help the searchers locate your position much more quickly.

A strobe light is another means of attracting attention from the air. MPI Outdoor Safety sells a lightweight strobe light that can be seen from up to three miles away. It is powered by one D-cell battery and flashes a 300,000 candlepower

A strobe light can help you to be seen for miles away.

strobe for up to sixty hours. This strobe is safe to use and can be quite effective in an emergency situation.

Still another way to attract the attention of aircraft from the ground is with a smoky fire. Pour water on a fire at a time when you think the smoke would be seen from the air.

The universal firearm signal for help is three shots fired at close and equal intervals. Whether or not you decide to carry a firearm, you should know this signal. Although the likelihood of attracting the attention of aircraft with three shots is slim, you may someday hear a series of shots that means someone close to you is in need of help.

If you use the tools of navigation wisely, however, your chances of ever becoming lost are slim.

True wilderness is shrinking as more outdoor people strike off on their own, and it is imperative that those of us who travel off the beaten path leave no mark in our passing. Each of us must take on this responsibility. The old saying "Leave nothing but footprints, take nothing but memories" is even more important now.

THE GLOBAL POSITIONING SYSTEM

The Global Positioning System (GPS) is something that you'll be hearing a lot about in the next few years. It's a worldwide system that can help you determine your position anywhere. The GPS navigational network is a constellation of satellites that was developed by the U.S. Department of Defense primarily as a military targeting and navigational system. The true effectiveness of this system was first proven during the Gulf War (Desert Storm), so the system is relatively new technology.

There presently are twenty-four GPS satellites orbiting the globe at an altitude of about 11,000 miles. These special satellites transmit high-frequency radio signals to the earth's surface, where any GPS receiver can lock on to the signal. A GPS receiver calculates position through triangulation and therefore must receive a beam from at least three satellites. Some GPS receivers gather signals from five or more satellites and can calculate elevation as well.

GPS receivers are currently available from a number of manufacturers (see Resources) and are designed to be carried in the field (or in a vehicle or boat.) These hand-held units have the ability to determine your position and indicate your speed of travel toward an objective. A GPS receiver can tell you, for example, how close you are to a small pond, lake, or cabin and how long it will take you to get there from your present position.

Hand-held GPS receivers cost quite a bit more than the

The Magellan Global Positioning System receiver can pinpoint your position in the wilds by picking up information from special satellites orbiting above the earth.

best compass available (prices range from about $500 to $1,700), but the possibilities for navigation are almost limitless. For instance, if you were to discover a small pond that was teeming with trout, you could determine its position with your GPS receiver and store this information in the unit. The next time you wanted to visit this special place, you could simply bring up the coordinates from the unit's memory, and your GPS receiver would show you the way back. Current accuracy is to within 10 meters.

The GPS system operates twenty-four hours a day and in any type of weather. If you are in the bottom of a steep canyon, you may have to climb to higher ground for your receiver to pick up signals, but the system should work in any other type of terrain or weather condition.

• RESOURCES •

CONSERVATION, HIKING, AND ENVIRONMENTAL ORGANIZATIONS

Adirondack Mountain Club, Inc. (ADK)
172 Ridge St.
Glens Falls, NY 12801
Trail guides, maps, and publications.

The American Hiking Society
P.O. Box 20160
Washington, DC 20041-2160

Appalachian Mountain Club (AMC)
5 Joy St.
Boston, MA 02108
Trail guides, maps, and publications.

Appalachian Trail Conference (ATC)
P.O. Box 236
Harpers Ferry, WV 25425
Appalachian Trail information.

Colorado Mountain Club (CMC)
2530 W. Alameda Ave.
Denver, CO 80219

Federation of Western Outdoor Clubs
4534½ University Way, N.E.
Seattle, WA 98105

Foundation for North American Wild Sheep
720 Allen Ave.
Cody, WY 82414
(307) 527-6261

National Audubon Society
950 Fifth Ave.
New York, NY 10028
National headquarters.

National Campers and Hikers Association
7172 Transit Rd.
Buffalo, NY 14221
Mainly for vehicular campers.

National Hiking and Ski Touring Association
P.O. Box 7421
Colorado Springs, CO 80907

The Nature Conservancy
1815 N. Linn St.
Arlington, VA 22209
(800) 628-6860

Pacific Northwest Trail Association
P.O. Box 1048
Seattle, WA 98111
Information on this multistate trail system.

Rocky Mountain Elk Foundation
P.O. Box 8249
Missoula, MT 59807
(800) 225-5355

Safari Club International
4800 W. Gates Pass Rd.
Tucson, AZ 85745
(602) 620-1220

Sierra Club
730 Polk St.
San Francisco, CA 94109
National headquarters.

The Wilderness Society
1901 Pennsylvania Ave., N.W.
Washington, DC 20006

Wildlife Forever
12301 Whitewater Dr., Suite 210
Minnetonka, MN 55343
(612) 936-0605
Wildlife habitat conservation and management.

Wildlife Legislative Fund of America
801 Kingsmill Pkwy.
Columbus, OH 43229-1137
(614) 888-4868
Sportsmen's rights organization.

GOVERNMENT AGENCIES—UNITED STATES

Bureau of Land Management
National Headquarters
1849 C St. NW, Suite #5600
Washington, DC 20240
(202) 208-5717
Manages 270 million acres of public lands, mainly in western states and Alaska.

State Directory
Alaska: 555 Cordova Street, Anchorage, AK 99501
Arizona: Federal Building, Phoenix, AZ 85025
California: Federal Building, 2800 Cottage Way, Sacramento, CA 95825
Colorado: Room 700, 1600 Broadway, Denver, CO 80202
Idaho: Federal Building., 550 W. Fort St., Boise, ID 83702
Montana, North Dakota, South Dakota, and Minnesota:
Federal Building, 316 N. 26th St., Billings, MT 59101
Nevada: Federal Building, Room 3008, 300 Booth St., Reno NV 89502
New Mexico and Oklahoma: Federal Building, South Federal Pl., Box 1449, Santa Fe, NM 87502
Oregon and Washington: 729 Northeast Oregon St., Box 2965, Portland, OR 97208
Utah: Federal Building, 125 South State, Salt Lake City, UT 84111
Wyoming, Nebraska, and Kansas: P.O. Box 1828, Cheyenne, WY 82001

Eastern States: 7981 Eastern Ave., Silver Spring, MD 20910
(covers all states not listed above)

Forest Service
National Headquarters
Forest Service
U.S. Department of Agriculture
14th St. and Independence Ave., S.W.
Washington, DC 20250

Regional Offices
Alaska: Box 1628, Juneau, AK 99801
California: 630 Sansome St., San Francisco, CA 94111
Colorado: Federal Center, Building 85, Denver, CO 80225
Georgia: 1720 Peachtree Rd., NW, Atlanta, GA 30309
Montana: Federal Building, Missoula, MT 59801
New Mexico: 517 Gold Ave., S.W., Albuquerque, NM 87101
Oregon: Box 3623, Portland, OR 97208
Utah: 324 25th St., Ogden, UT 84401
Wisconsin: 633 W. Wisconsin Ave., Milwaukee, WI 53203

National Park Service
Headquarters
National Park Service
Department of the Interior
C Street, between 18th & 19th Streets, N.W.
Washington, DC 20240
Information about national parks.

United States Geological Survey (USGS)
National Headquarters
U.S. Geological Survey
Map Information Office
National Center
Reston, VA 22092

Eastern Region
U.S. Geological Survey
Branch of Distribution
1200 South Eads St.
Arlington, VA 22202
Topographical maps and indexes for states east of the Mississippi River.

Western Region
U.S. Geological Survey
Branch of Distribution
Federal Center
Denver, CO 80225
Topographical maps and indexes for states west of the Mississippi River.

State Recreation and Tourism Bureaus

The following is a listing of the government agencies that provide information about parks, trails, wilderness areas, and fishing and hunting regulations throughout each state. Generally a good source of information.

Alabama: Bureau of Publicity and Information, Room 403, State Highway Building, Montgomery, AL 36104

Alaska: Travel Division, Pouch E, Juneau, AK 99891

Arizona: Office of Economic Planning and Development, Visitor Development Section, 1645 W. Jefferson St., Room 428, Phoenix, AZ 85007

Arkansas: Department of Parks and Tourism, 149 State Capitol, Little Rock, AR 72201

California: State Office of Tourism, 1400 Tenth St., Sacramento, CA 95814

Colorado: Division of Commerce and Development, 602 State Capitol Annex, Denver, CO 80203

Connecticut: Development Commission, State Office Building, Box 865, Hartford, CT 06115

Delaware: Division of Economic Development, 45 The Green, Dover, DE 19901

District of Columbia: Washington Convention and Visitors Bureau, 1129 20th St., N.W., Washington, DC 20036

Florida: Department of Commerce, Collins Building, 107 West Gaines Street, Tallahassee, FL 32304

Georgia: Department of Community Development, Box 38097, Atlanta, GA 30334

Hawaii: Visitors Bureau, 2270 Kalakaua Ave., Suite 801, Honolulu, HI 96815

Idaho: Division of Tourism, Room 108, State Capitol, Boise, ID 83720

Illinois: Department of Business and Economic Development, 205 West Wacker Dr., Suite 1122, Chicago, IL 60606

Indiana: Division of Tourism, Room 336, State House, Indianapolis, IN 46204

Iowa: Development Commission, Tourism and Travel Division, 250 Jewett Building, Des Moines, IA 50309

Kansas: Department of Economic Development, Room 122-S, State Office Building, Topeka, KS 66612

Kentucky: Department of Public Information, Capitol Annex, Frankfort, KY 40601

Louisiana: Tourist Commission, Box 44291, Baton Rouge, LA 70804

Maine: Department of Commerce and Industry, State House, Augusta, ME 04330

Maryland: Department of Economic and Community Development, 2525 Riva Road, Annapolis, MD 21401

Massachusetts: Department of Commerce and Development, 100 Cambridge St., Boston, MA 02202

Michigan: Tourist Council, 300 South Capitol Ave., Room 102, Lansing, MI 48926

Minnesota: Department of Economic Development, 480 Cedar St., Hanover Building, St. Paul, MN 55110

Mississippi: Agricultural and Industrial Board, 1504 State Office Building, Box 849, Jackson, MS 39205

Missouri: Division of Tourism, 308 East High St., Box 1055, Jefferson City, MO 65101

Montana: Department of Highways, Helena, MT 59601

Nebraska: Department of Economic Development, Box 94666, State Capitol, Lincoln, NE 68509

Nevada: Department of Economic Development, Travel-Tourism Division, Carson City, NV 89701

New Hampshire: Department of Economic Development, Vacation Travel Promotion, Box 856, Concord, NH 03301

New Jersey: Department of Economic Development, Department of Labor and Industry, Box 2766, Trenton, NJ 08625

New Mexico: Department of Development, Travel Bureau, 113 Washington Ave., Santa Fe, NM 87501

New York: State Department of Commerce, Travel Bureau, 99 Washington Ave., Albany, NY 12210

North Carolina: Department of Natural and Economic Resources, Travel and Promotion, Box 27685, Raleigh, NC 27611

North Dakota: Highway Department, Capitol Grounds, Bismarck, ND 58501

Ohio: Department of Economic and Community Development, 30 East Broad St., Columbus, OH 43215

Oklahoma: Tourism and Recreation Division, 500 Will Rogers Building, Oklahoma City, OK 73105

Oregon: Travel Information Section, 104 State Highway Building, Salem, OR 97310

Pennsylvania: Department of Commerce, Bureau of Travel Development, 431 South Office Building, Harrisburg, PA 17120

Rhode Island: Department of Economic Development, Tourism, One Weybosset Hill, Providence, RI 02903

South Carolina: Department of Parks, Recreation and Tourism, Box 113, 1205 Pendleton St., Columbia, SC 29201

South Dakota: Department of Economic and Tourism Development, Division of Tourism, Pierre, SD 57501

Tennessee: Tourism Development, 1007 Andrew Jackson State Office Building, Nashville, TN 37211

Texas: Travel and Information Division, Highway Department, Austin, TX 78701

Utah: Travel Council, Council Hill, Capitol Hill, Salt Lake City, UT 84114

Vermont: Agency of Development and Community Affairs, Information—Travel Development, 61 Elm St., Montpelier, VT 05602

Virginia: State Travel Service, 6 North Sixth St., Richmond, VA 23219

Washington: Department of Commerce and Economic Development, General Administration Building, Olympia, WA 98504

West Virginia: Department of Commerce, Travel Development Division, Room B-533, 1900 Washington St. E., Charleston, WV 25305

Wisconsin: Department of Natural Resources, Vacation and Travel Development, Box 450, Madison, WI 53701

Wyoming: Travel Commission, 2320 Capitol Ave., Cheyenne, WY 82002

GOVERNMENT AGENCIES—CANADA

Canada Map Office
Department of Energy
Mines and Resources
Ottawa, Ontario, Canada K1A OE9
The source for all Canadian topographical maps; send for index of provinces.

Canadian Government Travel Bureau
150 Kent St.
Ottawa, Ontario, Canada K1A OH6

OUTDOOR-EQUIPMENT MANUFACTURERS

Bausch & Lomb Sports Optics Division
9200 Cody
Overland Park, KS 66214
(800) 423-3537

The Brunton Company
620 East Monroe
Riverton, WY 82501-4997
(800) 443-4871

Cabela's, Inc.
812 13th Ave.
Sidney, NE 69160-0001
(800) 331-3454

Cascade Designs, Inc.
4000 First Ave. S.
Seattle, WA 98134
(206) 583-0583

The Coleman Company
P.O. Box 2931
250 N. St. Francis
Wichita, KS 67201
(316) 261-3367

Columbia Sportswear Company
P.O. Box 83239
6600 North Baltimore
Portland, OR 97283-0239
(800) 622-6953

Danner Shoe Manufacturing Co.
12722 N.E. Airport Way
Portland, OR 97230
(503) 251-1100

DeLorme Mapping Company
P.O. Box 298
Freeport, Maine 04032
(800) 227-1656
Topographical map atlases for twenty-six states.

Eagle Electronics
P.O. Box 669
Catoosa, OK 74015-0669
(800) 324-4737
Accunav Sport global positioning system (GPS) receivers.

Garmin
9875 Widmer Rd.
Lenexa, KS 66125
GPS75 global positioning system receivers.

Gore-Tex Fabrics
100 Airport Rd., Building 2
P.O. Box 729
Elkton, MD 21922-0729
(800) 431-GORE

Jansport
10411 Airport Rd.
Everett, WA 98204
(800) 552-6776
Outdoor equipment and clothing.

Kampgrounds of America, Inc.
P.O. Box 30558
Billings, MT 59114
(406) 248-7444
KOA annual guide to campgrounds.

L. L. Bean, Inc.
Casco Street
Freeport, ME 04033
(800) 221-4221
Outdoor clothing and equipment.

Lowrance Electronics, Inc.
12000 East Skelly Dr.
Tulsa, OK 74128-2486
(800) 324-4737
Eagle GPS navigational units.

Magellan Systems Corp.
960 Overland Ct.
San Dimas, CA 91773
(800) 669-4477
Trailblazer GPS receivers.

Micrologic SuperSport
9610 DeSoto Ave.
Chatsworth, CA 91311
SuperSport GPS receivers.

MPI Outdoor Safety
85 Flagship Dr., Suite D
North Andover, MA 01845
(508) 685-2700
Space blankets, strobelights, and other outdoor safety products.

Nikon Sport Optics
19601 Hamilton Ave.
Torrance, CA 90502
(800) NIKON-US
Binoculars, cameras, lenses.

The Orvis Company, Inc.
River Road
Manchester, VT 05254
(800) 815-5900
Fishing gear.

Panasonic
1 Panasonic Way
Secaucus, NJ 07094
Panasonic KX-G5500 GPS receivers.

Pendleton Woolen Mills
P.O. Box 3030
Portland, OR 97208
(503) 226-4801
Outdoor clothing.

PUR
Division of Recovery Engineering, Inc.
2229 Edgewood Ave. S.
Minneapolis, MN 55426
(612) 541-1313
Water purifiers and filters.

REI
Dept. 4127
Summer, WA 98352-0001
(800) 426-4840

Rocky Shoes & Boots, Inc.
Rocky Telemarketing Center
Hocking Technical College
Nelsonville, OH 45764
(800) 421-5151
Boots.

Sherpa, Inc.
444 S. Pine
Burlington, WI 53105
Snowshoes.

Silva Orienteering Services
P.O. Box 547
La Porte, IN 46350

Sony
1 Sony Dr.
Park Ridge, NJ 07656
Sony Pyxis IPS-760 GPS receivers.

3M Company
Insulation & Specialty Fabrics
3M Center Bldg.
275-6W-01
St. Paul, MN 55144
(800) 328-1689
Consumer information.

Tender Corp.
P.O. Box 290
Littleton Industrial Park
Littleton, NH 03561
(603) 444-5464

Trails Illustrated
P.O. Box 3610
Evergreen, CO 80439
(800) 962-1643
Waterproof (plastic-coated) topographical maps.

Trimble Scout GPS
9020-11 Capitol of Texas Hwy. N.
Austin, TX 78759
Trimble Scout GPS receivers.

• GLOSSARY •

azimuth: a degree bearing from your position to an objective.

back bearing: the return bearing from an objective.

base plate: the rectangular plate of an orienteering compass on which the compass housing is mounted.

bearing: a direction of travel expressed in degrees from 1 to 360.

cardinal points: the four principal points of a compass: north, south, east, and west.

checkpoint: a prominent or conspicuous land feature shown on a map and used to check progress.

compass: an instrument for determining direction (expressed in degree readings) that consists of a magnetized strip of steel swinging and pointing toward magnetic north.

contour interval: the difference in height between one contour line and the one next to it, expressed in feet.

contour line: an imaginary line in the field along which every point is the same height above sea level. Used on topographical maps to indicate elevation.

cultural features: man-made landscape features as shown on a topographical map, such as roads, buildings, and airports.

declination: the difference in degrees between the direction a compass needle points (magnetic north) and true north at any given location.

dial: the rim or edge of a compass housing, marked with degrees from 1 to 360 and the cardinal points of north, south, east, and west.

direction: the relative location of a landscape feature from a present position. (See also *bearing*).

direction-of-travel arrow: the arrow embossed on the base plate of an orienteering compass; indicates the direction of travel to an objective once the compass has been oriented to magnetic north.

housing: that part of a compass that contains the magnetic needle and a damping fluid. A compass housing can be rotated 360 degrees.

hydrographic features: water features on a topographical map, both man-made and natural, such as ponds, lakes, reservoirs, and streams.

index pointer: the line on the raised part of the base plate on an orienteering compass against which the degree reading on the dial can be read.

intercardinal points: those four points on a compass between the four cardinal points: northeast, southeast, southwest, and northwest.

landmark: any feature in the landscape that can be easily recognized, such as a prominent tree, rock, dwelling, or lake.

latitude: the distance in degrees north and south from the equator.

longitude: the distance in degrees east and west from Greenwich, England.

magnetic lines: lines drawn on a topographical map by the user to indicate the direction of magnetic north.

magnetic north: that geographical location to which all (unadjusted) compass needles point.

map: a scale representation of a section of the earth's surface.

map symbols: representative marks used on a map to indicate various features on the landscape, such as dwellings, roads, swamps, or trails.

meridians: lines on a printed map that indicate true north and true south.

orientation: the process of determining one's position in the field with the aid of one or more of the following: a map, compass, land features, or a global positioning system.

orienteering: the act of navigating in the field with the aid of map and compass.

orienteering compass: a compass designed to simplify the process of finding your way with map and compass. The most common types have a clear, rectangular plastic base plate and a compass housing that can be rotated in use.

orienting (a map): rotating a topographical (or other) map in the field so that it corresponds with magnetic north and visible land features.

orienting arrow: an arrow embossed in the housing of an orienteering compass and used for setting the compass.

orienting lines of compass: the lines inside the bottom of a compass housing parallel to the north-south orienting arrow.

protractor: an instrument used for determining and measuring angles in degrees; commonly made from clear plastic.

quadrangle: a rectangular section of land depicted on a topographical map.

route: the path taken between two given points.

scale: the proportion between actual distance in the field and distance on a map. Commonly expressed as a ratio, such as 1:25,000, which indicates that 1 inch on the map equals 25,000 inches actual distance.

topographical maps: maps produced by the United States Geological Survey, of high quality and a major tool for traveling in the wilderness.